Copyright 2024 Mike Perron.
All rights reserved.
No part of this book may be reproduced in any form or by any electronic or mechanical means including information storage and retrieval systems without written permission from the publisher, except by a reviewer, who may quote brief passages in a review.
First printing, 2024.
ISBN: 979-8-35094-695-6

236 DIFFERENT WAYS TO WRITE THE SAME AD

by Mike Perron

"Simplicity is the ultimate sophistication."
Leonardo Da Vinci

"There isn't any significant difference between the various brands of whiskey, or cigarettes or beer. They are all about the same. And so are the cake mixes and the detergents, and the margarines... The manufacturer who dedicates his advertising to building the most sharply defined personality for his brand will get the largest share of the market at the highest profit."
David Ogilvy,
The Father of Advertising

"Great advertising is never bound by a small budget."
Mike Perron

INTRODUCTION

I own a paint store on the island of St. Thomas in the U.S. Virgin Islands. It was opened the first week of April in 1995. Population in our market, about 60,000 on an island that's 14 miles long by 4 miles wide.

Before moving there, I sold advertising space in newspapers and magazines, been a copywriter, promotion manager at a large department store, associate publisher for a magazine to name a few jobs.

I've been laid off a few times, fired twice and quit 17 jobs by the time I was 38. Then I thought, gee, I'll start my own business and make lots of money for myself.

The first business I started was with a partner. A boat business. In the late 80's when interest rates climbed to over 20%, our business, as well as thousands of other businesses went bankrupt. Broke, no job, in debt, I made my way to St. Thomas where my other half, Linda Rayner, was working as a singer for a three month stint.

I got a job as a painter. Eight bucks per hour. Believe me, my hands had never done physical work much less seen a paint brush. But, you gotta do what you gotta do to survive. Depressed at my situation? Not at all.

Within three months, I bought the painting business from the guy I was working for as he decided to move back to Florida. Two thousand dollars got me a beat up pick up truck, one old airless paint sprayer, two ladders, no employees and one contact.

I grew the business into a 35 employee paint contracting business. And I advertised. I was the only paint contractor advertising. It got to the point where I was purchasing a great deal of paint. So much so that I thought I might as well open up my own paint

THE PAINT DEPOT

Coatings for every surface from the most knowledgeable and service oriented paint people.
AT THE TOP OF RAPHUNE HILL, ST. THOMAS, VIRGIN ISLANDS. 775-1466

store.

Within a year of opening up the store, I wound down the paint contracting business. All the leads and contacts I had acquired, I then passed on to my former competitors or former paint employees who started their own painting business. And of course as a thank you for the leads, they bought paint from me.

We were profitable every single year from when we opened in 1995 and remain today, 2023, a highly profitable company.

How profitable? I was recently looking at Shopify statistics on industry profitability per employee for 2022. In the retail category, The Paint Depot is more than *10 times more profitable* per employee than the average retailer in the US.

In this business, in this closed market place, the only way to increase market share was to take it away from someone else. And that meant promoting and advertising.

We spent more in advertising than all the other paint store competitors combined. I wish I was able to use more co-op dollars from our paint suppliers but they have rules on how their ads can be designed. If you've ever seen any, and I mean any major paint manufacturing advertising, you'll know that you could interchange the logo with any other ad and no one would know the difference. I wanted to stand out.

Here was my advertising belief for my store, in this market. People won't read paint ads unless they are *actually* in the market to buy paint. Sort of like tire ads. You don't notice them until you realize your tires are getting bald and you need new ones. So, I needed to advertise with great frequency because I didn't know when people would be thinking of painting.

"DOWN BOY, <u>DOWN!</u>"

THE PAINT DEPOT

Coatings for every surface from the most knowledgeable and service oriented paint people.

AT THE TOP OF RAPHUNE HILL, ST. THOMAS, VIRGIN ISLANDS. 775-1466

Second, I had to get people to read the ads. So they had to be catchy and of course, sell as well. Hence the blind headlines on a lot of my ads. They draw people in. It's always a nice extra if you can reward the reader with a little twist in the copy. They'll enjoy reading it.

Third, like a comic strip with a large following, I needed to place my ads in the same place, same time, week in and week out. All of this would create better awareness.

We ran five column by 4 inch ads, black & white on Mondays in the local daily paper. It always ran on page 4 or 5. In any case, it was always the first live ad in the newspaper. We also ran an ad, same size, in the TV listing insert of the Saturday edition of the newspaper.

For the last ten years, our ads now run on page 2 of the newspaper on Mondays and Wednesdays. We are the only ad on a two page editorial spread.

And the results? We sell more paint than anyone else. For the first ten years, we only carried the Martin Senour brand of paint. Of the over 2,000 dealers in the US at the time, we were the top producer. *Every single year.*

So, in no particular order, here are the ads that made this store #1 every year.

I hope they inspire you to do the same with your business.

Mike Perron,
St. Thomas, Virgin Islands.

ANATOMY OF OUR ADS.

As I indicated earlier, if you're not interested in paint, you won't be interested in the ad. But, what if you found the headline amusing or intriguing? You might just linger long enough to catch the name of our company.

You might not need paint now, but I've introduced myself to you. Eventually, a year or two or even three down the way, I've put 150 different headlines in front of you. So when it's your time to buy paint or roof coatings, I think The Paint Depot will come to mind.

Ninety percent of my ads look like this. Big bold outline with a bold headline. A bold logo and our slogan. Then copy that narrates a story while selling and entertaining.

The vast majority of our ads have no product photos so the words do all the work. We promote the brand, "The Paint Depot" first, not the paint suppliers.

The premise of this ad is, when painting cabinets, you want to avoid brush marks. You want the paint to lay down smoothly. Benjamin Moore Impervo enamel paint does just that, it lays down without brush marks. Now, let's sell that creatively.

I use the dog analogy and copy twists four times in the body copy. It's simple, fun, and tells you what this product does.

In addition to the daily newspaper, we ran this ad in the St. Thomas Humane Society fund raising book.

"DOWN BOY, DOWN!"

Getting a paint to lay down smoothly when brushing can be dogs work. Fortunately, there's Benjamin-Moore Impervo alkyd enamel in high gloss and low lustre. I haven't found a single professional painter who didn't wag his tail at the way this paint flows off the brush and lays down so obediently. If you are planning to paint cabinets, doors or trim and have always used the other guys paint, then it's time you come in and try Benjamin-Moore Impervo enamel. Who knows, you just might learn a new painting trick.

THE PAINT DEPOT

Coatings for every surface from the most knowledgeable and service oriented paint people.
AT THE TOP OF RAPHUNE HILL, ST. THOMAS, VIRGIN ISLANDS. 775-1466

WORDS, WORDS, WORDS.
WHICH ONES SHOULD I USE.

Because our ads are all copy, the words take on a major importance. There are no visuals.

My first copywriting job was at large insurance company back in 1972. I was 21. The pay was terrible, the rules in the office were petty.

I was in a very large room in a sea of desks all arranged in a grid pattern. Probably about 50 of us in there. The title of my boss was "Assistant Vice President in Charge of Advertising". I was his assistant. Everyone else in the room was an assistant to someone else either creating insurance policies, paying out insurance policies or typing letters for whomever they were assisting.

No one was allowed to talk. No one had a phone on their desk. I was the only one given a phone since I had to deal with printers for the brochures. It was also a party line with my boss. I had to go to his office and let him know I was about to use the phone.

I stayed there 5 months before moving on to another job that paid two and a half times more. However, I learned a very valuable lesson about copywriting.

My job was to write brochures to sell insurance. I was given the legal insurance policy document and had to write something that ordinary people could understand and find beneficial enough to buy it. The first time I went into his office to present the copy I had just written, he didn't even look at my work. He simply stared at me and said "Tell me, are you happy with it?" I took the copy, went back to my desk and started rewriting.

It's where I learned you need to write, rewrite over and over again. This is what copywriting is about. To rewrite

THIS COLOR STINKS!

Actually, you really like the color. It's the paint that stinks. If you're very sensitive to paint odor or you need to paint an office, hotel room or other public area that you can't close down, try our Benjamin Moore EcoSpec paint. An hour later, your nose won't be able to tell that the room was ever painted! So now, when someone tells you the color stinks, you can only blame your decorator.

THE PAINT DEPOT
Coatings for every surface from the most knowledgeable and service oriented paint people.
AT THE TOP OF RAPHUNE HILL, ST. THOMAS, VIRGIN ISLANDS. 775-1466

until you can't change, add or delete a single word.

It wasn't uncommon to rewrite a simple paragraph 15 times. So later, when I handed in my copy and he asked that question, I could say "Yes, I'm happy with it."

Every great copywriter who has ever existed will say you need to write. All the time.

When I first started, I'd take ads that I thought were brilliant and just hand write them out in longhand. I did that over and over again. I don't think it's any different than a musician playing some else's music that they thought was brilliant.

To create your own stuff, you need to understand what great stuff is.

$1,267.20 PER GALLON!

My wife's nail polish costs $4.95 for half an ounce.
Which puts the cost of one gallon of nail polish at $1,267.20!
I'm not saying you should buy our Great Life exterior latex semi-gloss
for your finger nails, but I am saying it doesn't cost
much to get the very best quality paint.
Now, we've got inexpensive paints as well, but when
you're painting exterior surfaces, two coats of paint
(which is only about .004 inches thick)
is supposed to protect your home from the salt air,
the tropical sun and strong wind driven rain.
With our Great Life paint, you'll be getting the best
quality coating for your walls for about
$1,242.04 *less* than a gallon of nail polish.
And the nice thing is,
our Great Life paint is as tough as nails.

THE PAINT DEPOT

Coatings for every surface from the most knowledgeable and service oriented paint people.

AT THE TOP OF RAPHUNE HILL, ST. THOMAS, VIRGIN ISLANDS. 775-1466 OR 775-0429

PURCHASE OF A COMPETITOR.

In 2004, one of our competitors, Mike's Paint Store, decided to sell their business. They were a Benjamin Moore paint dealer in the Virgin Islands for 27 years. We didn't buy their location, just the rights to sell Benjamin Moore and their inventory.

Coincidentally, my name is Mike as well, so we played with that too.

Here is a series of 6 ads we used to promote the acquisition and transition to our location.

LOOKING FOR BENJAMIN MOORE PAINT? GO TO MIKE'S!

Mike Perron of The Paint Depot that is. We are now the official Benjamin-Moore paint dealer for St. Thomas and St. John. All the super products you've come to love are of course still here, like Martin-Senour paint, Zinsser mildew proof paint, Vulkem and ToughKote roof coatings. It's just that now, with the world's best paints, best roof coatings, best service and best color selection all under one roof, there's just no mistaking where to shop. Mike's place.

THE PAINT DEPOT

Coatings for every surface from the most knowledgeable and service oriented paint people.
AT THE TOP OF RAPHUNE HILL, ST. THOMAS, VIRGIN ISLANDS. 775-1466

AND FULL PAGES, TOO.

In addition to our regular sized ads, we often would boost our advertising with full pages in the newspaper.

No matter the size, we kept the design element the same.

HELP ME LOSE 62,000 LBS OF WEIGHT.

Believe me, moving the contents of Mike's Paint Store into our existing location is like putting 7 quarts of paint into a 1 gallon can. Even with 6,500 sq. ft. of space, we need to lose a little weight. And that means BIG savings to you. We've put everything in the store on sale from 10% to 75% off! How about Benjamin-Moore latex caulk, reg. $3.95 a tube now .98 cents, save 75%! Or check out Linzzer professional paint brushes, 3" nylon blend reg. $15.00 now $3.75, save 75%! All Martin-Senour Platinum paint, 40% off! I don't think I need to say hurry! But I need to tell you that this one-time mega sale ends Dec. 15th. Quantities limited.

THE PAINT DEPOT

Coatings for every surface from the most knowledgeable and service oriented paint people.
AT THE TOP OF RAPHUNE HILL, ST. THOMAS, VIRGIN ISLANDS. 775-1466 OR 775-0429

WE TOOK OVER THEIR PHONE NUMBER AS WELL.

Right after we purchased our competitor, I called the phone company and bought their phone number and put it on call forward to our number.

775-0429

Yes, I know this is not our number, it's the old Mike's Paint Store phone number. But since a lot of their customers had spent over 25 years memorizing it, we decided to make things easier for them to get their Benjamin-Moore paint. So, for the rest of the year, when you dial that old number, it'll ring right here at The Paint Depot. We just didn't pick up a beautiful paint line, we also picked up a cute little number.

THE PAINT DEPOT

Coatings for every surface from the most knowledgeable and service oriented paint people.
AT THE TOP OF RAPHUNE HILL, ST. THOMAS, VIRGIN ISLANDS. 775-1466 OR 775-0429

WE DECIDED TO MAKE YOUR NEXT VISIT HERE MORE DIFFICULT.

Two thousand colors. You'd think that would be enough choices. But noooooooooo!!! Someone had to go and add all the colors of Benjamin-Moore in addition to the Martin-Senour colors at The Paint Depot. Now there's over 5000 colors to choose from! Hey, wait a minute! Did you say Benjamin-Moore paint is now available at The Paint Depot? Yep! We are now the official Benjamin-Moore paint dealer in St. Thomas and St. John. More paint, more colors, more service. What could be easier?

THE PAINT DEPOT

Coatings for every surface from the most knowledgeable and service oriented paint people.
AT THE TOP OF RAPHUNE HILL, ST. THOMAS, VIRGIN ISLANDS. 775-1466 OR 775-0429

IT'S REALLY CROWDED HERE SO WE'RE HAVING A BIG SALE.

After buying Mike's Paint store, you can imagine what it's like to try and put 12,000 gallons of extra paint into our place. So we need to move out extra inventory. And to make it worth your while, we're putting everything in the store on sale from 10% to 75% off! How about Benjamin-Moore latex caulk, reg. $3.95 a tube, now .98 cents, save 75%! Or check out Linzzer professional paint brushes, 3 inch nylon blend reg. $15.00 now $3.75, save 75%!
Do I need to say hurry!
Sale ends Dec. 15th. Quantities are limited.

THE PAINT DEPOT

Coatings for every surface from the most knowledgeable and service oriented paint people.
AT THE TOP OF RAPHUNE HILL, ST. THOMAS, VIRGIN ISLANDS. 775-1466 OR 775-0429

AND THE NUMBER 1 REASON WHY...

I got the idea for this ad watching The David Letterman Show. Each night he'd have a Top Ten list segment which was quite funny.

TOP TEN REASONS WHY I ADDED THE BENJAMIN-MOORE PAINT LINE TO OUR STORE.

Number 10: I thought it would be fun to cram an extra 12,000 gallons of paint into our existing store.

Number 9: I needed something else to write ads about.

Number 8: I felt inadequate with only one brand of paint.

Number 7: It was the only way to get that bunch of hardcore Benjamin-Moore paint users to shop in my store.

Number 6: The Fab Five in New York use Benjamin-Moore paint.

Number 5: Martin-Senour paint and Benjamin-Moore paint are both hyphenated words.

Number 4: I can now tell people that my inventory is bigger than theirs.

Number 3: Someone once told me Moore is better.

Number 2: Benjamin is the name of my favorite nephew.

And the **Number 1** reason why I added the Benjamin-Moore line of paint to our store... I wanted to make it more difficult for our customers by having over 5,000 colors to choose from instead of only 2000.

THE PAINT DEPOT

Coatings for every surface from the most knowledgeable and service oriented paint people.

AT THE TOP OF RAPHUNE HILL, ST. THOMAS, VIRGIN ISLANDS. 775-1466 OR 775-0429

IF YOU'RE LOOKING FOR BENJAMIN MOORE PAINTS WHO YA GONNA CALL?

Surprised? So are we! We've always wanted to have this great line of paints. So when we got the opportunity to become the new dealer for St. Thomas and St. John, we of course said yes! All the super products you've come to love are of course still available, like Martin Senour paints, Vulkem roof coating, ToughKote roof coating and Zinsser mildew proof paint. It's just that now with the world's best paints, best roof coatings, best service and best color selection all under one roof, you just *know* who to call.

THE PAINT DEPOT

Coatings for every surface from the most knowledgeable and service oriented paint people.
AT THE TOP OF RAPHUNE HILL, ST. THOMAS, VIRGIN ISLANDS. 775-1466

50% OF OUR STAFF IS ACTUALLY LEFT HANDED.

One day I realized that 50% of our staff was left handed. Well, there's always a way to weave an interesting fact into a Paint Depot ad.

HOW IS IT THAT 50% OF OUR STAFF IS LEFT HANDED?

With less than 15% of the regular population left handed, how is it that our staff is neatly divided between left and right handed people?
Well, there was a good reason why we hired our people this way.
You see, on one hand we are very liberal with our low prices and on the other hand we are very conservative when it comes to selecting great products. But when it comes to giving great service, we become bipartisan and give you the benefit of both our left and right-handed thinking.

THE PAINT DEPOT

Coatings for every surface from the most knowledgeable and service oriented paint people.
AT THE TOP OF RAPHUNE HILL, ST. THOMAS, VIRGIN ISLANDS. 775-1466

MIRACLE PRIMER.

Boy, I sure wish there was one. But there isn't. Which is why we carry more primers than anyone else, 43 of them at last count. So the next time you're in buying paint and we ask you what surface you're painting, it's because if you need a primer, we want to recommend the one best suited for your purpose. Right now, 5 gallons of Stretchcoat Acrylic masonry primer is on sale for $78.00, a 25% savings. Proline interior drywall primer, reg. $69.95 for 5 gal., has been reduced to $45.47, a 35% savings. Great products, incredible service AND low prices. It's not a miracle, it's The Paint Depot.

THE PAINT DEPOT

Coatings for every surface from the most knowledgeable and service oriented paint people.
AT THE TOP OF RAPHUNE HILL, ST. THOMAS, VIRGIN ISLANDS. 775-1466

PHYSICALLY ENGAGING THE READER.

Here is a different kind of 'call to action' for an ad.

This one ran on the bottom of a right hand page in the newspaper. The second part of the ad ran on the very next page on the bottom of the left hand page. When you turn this page, you'll see the effect of the ad and how the copy ties in.

Freedom, inhibits creativity. There's nothing like restrictions to get you thinking. If you've ever been asked to solve a problem with a small budget or a tight deadline, you've probably found that you were much more resourceful than if you had been given lots of money and time. That's because limits force us to think beyond conventional solutions.

Composer, Stephen Sondheim said, "if you ask me to write a song about the ocean, I'm stumped. But if you tell me to write a ballad about a woman in a red dress falling off her stool at three in the morning, I'm inspired." Creativity allows us to make "mental leaps." Voltaire said that "there isn't a problem anywhere in the world that can withstand the assault of sustained thinking." If I could correct him I'd say "sustained *creative* thinking"

STICK YOUR FINGER RIGHT THROUGH

THIS SPOT...
...and then turn the page. (No peeking first!)

When it comes to patching any kind of holes, you'll find everything you need right here. We've got DAP and Zinsser brand vinyl spackling compound, in regular and light weight formula, for patching plaster and drywall holes. You'll also find DAP plastic wood putty for, you guessed it, wood holes. Got holes in your stained wood? Use our Minwax wood putty that has been color matched to Minwax wood stains. Big concrete holes? Try our quick dry hydraulic cement. Now, if you have really long holes in your masonry (some people call them cracks), then you'll want to use our Benjamin-Moore textured brush grade and knife grade patching compound. A small hole in your car? Hey, we won't ask how you got it, but we do have a variety of automotive bodyfillers to patch it up. And don't worry if you're short on dough. Our prices, on the whole, are always very, very good.

THE PAINT DEPOT

Coatings for every surface from the most knowledgeable and service oriented paint people.

AT THE TOP OF RAPHUNE HILL, ST. THOMAS, VIRGIN ISLANDS. 775-1466

TESTIMONIALS FROM OUR CUSTOMERS.

Martin-Senour paint ran a campaign in the U.S. using golfer Chi Chi Rodriguez as their spokesperson. We never used Chi Chi or the ad material from their stateside ad agency down here. However, they used a line that I thought had potential, "These guys know paint like I know golf." We adapted the line to tie in with actual Paint Depot customers and their businesses.

Endorsement cost: zero dollars. And a win-win for us and the local businesses featured.

"THESE GUYS KNOW PAINT LIKE I KNOW A HOLE IN THE GROUND."

Gerry Roy, President,
Roy's Construction and Excavating

THE PAINT DEPOT

Coatings for every surface from the most knowledgeable and service oriented paint people.
AT THE TOP OF RAPHUNE HILL, ST. THOMAS, VIRGIN ISLANDS. 775-1466

"THESE GUYS ARE SO HELPFUL NO MATTER HOW MUCH I TAX THEIR PATIENCE."

Katherine Gibson, PC,
Tax Preparation & Accounting Services

THE PAINT DEPOT

Coatings for every surface from the most knowledgeable and service oriented paint people.
AT THE TOP OF RAPHUNE HILL, ST. THOMAS, VIRGIN ISLANDS. 775-1466

"THESE GUYS MAKE CUSTOM PAINT COLOR MATCHING COMPLETELY PAINLESS."

Henry E. Karlin, DDS,
The Smile Center

THE PAINT DEPOT

Coatings for every surface from the most knowledgeable and service oriented paint people.

AT THE TOP OF RAPHUNE HILL, ST. THOMAS, VIRGIN ISLANDS. 775-1466

"THESE GUYS KNOW PAINT LIKE I KNOW THE BACK OF MY HAND."

Linda Rayner,
Tarot and Palm Reading

THE PAINT DEPOT
Coatings for every surface from the most knowledgeable and service oriented paint people.
AT THE TOP OF RAPHUNE HILL, ST. THOMAS, VIRGIN ISLANDS. 775-1466

"THESE GUYS MAKE YOU FEEL GREAT EVEN WHEN YOU'RE DOWN IN THE DUMPS."

Peter Caproni, President
Y.E.S. Trash Removal

THE PAINT DEPOT

Coatings for every surface from the most knowledgeable and service oriented paint people.
AT THE TOP OF RAPHUNE HILL, ST. THOMAS, VIRGIN ISLANDS. 775-1466

"THESE GUYS WILL GIVE YOU GREAT SERVICE UNTIL THE COWS COME HOME."

Fred Hintz, President,
St. Thomas Dairies

THE PAINT DEPOT

Coatings for every surface from the most knowledgeable and service oriented paint people.
AT THE TOP OF RAPHUNE HILL, ST. THOMAS, VIRGIN ISLANDS. 775-1466

"THESE GUYS CAN MATCH PAINT COLORS LIKE I CAN SIZE YOU UP TO A 'T'."

Bill D'Ambrosia, President,
Billy D's T-Shirt Factory

THE PAINT DEPOT

Coatings for every surface from the most knowledgeable and service oriented paint people.
AT THE TOP OF RAPHUNE HILL, ST. THOMAS, VIRGIN ISLANDS. 775-1466

"THESE GUYS KNOW ROOF COATINGS LIKE I KNOW _ _ _ _."

Lew Henley, President,
Lew Henley Sewage Disposal

THE PAINT DEPOT

Coatings for every surface from the most knowledgeable and service oriented paint people.
AT THE TOP OF RAPHUNE HILL, ST. THOMAS, VIRGIN ISLANDS. 775-1466

"THESE GUYS WERE SO GOOD, IT MADE QUITE AN IMPRESSION ON ME."

Jimmy Buffam, President
Jimmy Buffam Tattoos

THE PAINT DEPOT

Coatings for every surface from the most knowledgeable and service oriented paint people.
AT THE TOP OF RAPHUNE HILL, ST. THOMAS, VIRGIN ISLANDS. 775-1466

"THESE GUYS KNOW PAINT LIKE I'M WAY OUT OF MY DEPTH."

Chris Sawyer, President
Chris Sawyer Diving Center

THE PAINT DEPOT

Coatings for every surface from the most knowledgeable and service oriented paint people.
AT THE TOP OF RAPHUNE HILL, ST. THOMAS, VIRGIN ISLANDS. 775-1466

THINKING OUTSIDE THE RECTANGLE.

This type of ad has been done before but its effectiveness is not diminished. When seen as a newspaper ad surrounded by live editorial, you really stand out.

THIS MILDEW IS DRIVING ME UP THE WAL!

The rainy season is just around the corner. And that means serious mildew growth for everyone living up in the hills.
Fortunately, there's Zinsser Perma-White mildew proof paint. Notice we said 'mildew proof' not 'mildew resistant'. There's a big difference.
This is the only house paint guaranteed to prevent mildew growth for 5 years when two coats are applied according to label directions.
Oh, by the way, if prices are also driving you up the wall,
you'll be pleased to know that we sell Zinsser PermaWhite paint for less than anyone on island.

THE PAINT DEPOT

Coatings for every surface from the most knowledgeable and service oriented paint people.
AT THE TOP OF RAPHUNE HILL, ST. THOMAS, VIRGIN ISLANDS. 775-1466

PLAYING WITH YOUR NAME.

I've been staring at our business name for years. Then I started removing letters from the word 'paint' one at a time. And this series of ads is what came out of it.

They ran on sequential bottom, right hand pages in the same issue of the local daily newspaper.

We ain't slow.
We ain't expensive
We ain't out of stuff.
And we sure ain't mean.

THE AINT DEPOT
Coatings for every surface from the most knowledgeable and service oriented paint people.
AT THE TOP OF RAPHUNE HILL, ST. THOMAS, VIRGIN ISLANDS. 775-1466

G'day! We can sell you a pint of Martin-Senour automotive finish, a two pint can of Benjamin-Moore house paint, an eight pint can of Zinsser mildew proof paint or a forty pint container of Vulkem roof coating.

THE P INT DEPOT

Coatings for every surface from the most knowledgeable and service oriented paint people.
AT THE TOP OF RAPHUNE HILL, ST. THOMAS, VIRGIN ISLANDS. 775-1466

Looking for those heavy duty, triple stitched painter's pants? We've got a great selection of them in waist sizes from 30" to 38". Prefer the shorts version? We got 'em too.

THE PA NT DEPOT

Coatings for every surface from the most knowledgeable and service oriented paint people.
AT THE TOP OF RAPHUNE HILL, ST. THOMAS, VIRGIN ISLANDS. 775-1466

I'D LIKE TO BUY THE LETTER "T".

During a minor hurricane, the letter "T" blew off our sign on our building leaving the name "The Pain Depot".

I left it like that until I could run this ad again.

If you find it painful to sand, scrape, climb a tall ladder or lift heavy five gallon buckets of Benjamin-Moore and Martin-Senour paint, then come on it. We've got everything you need to make it worse.

THE PAIN DEPOT

Coatings for every surface from the most knowledgeable and service oriented paint people.

LOOK MA, NO LOGO!

The Paint Depot enjoys incredible brand awareness. Not many retailers can remove their logos or names and still have brand recognition. Ninety percent of our ads have the same design element. Five columns wide, four inches high. Black & White. And they run on page 2 of the local daily newspaper (Mondays and Wednesdays.)

The "Who Ya Gonna Call?" ad ran when the movie Ghost Busters was playing. The song 'Ghost Busters' was so catchy and recognizable, that reading this ad would create what I call 'imagery transfer". Meaning, as you read the words in the ad, you'd start saying them in tune with the song.

WHEN YOUR ROOF IS LEAKING OR YOUR PAINT IS PEELING,

WHO YA GONNA CALL?

(Fill in the blanks below and then shout out loud.)

Coatings for every surface from the most knowledgeable and service oriented paint people.
AT THE TOP OF RAPHUNE HILL, ST. THOMAS, VIRGIN ISLANDS. 775-1466

DIALING FOR DOLLARS!

Calling any other competitor phone number will connect you to higher prices for a gallon of
Zinsser's Perma White mildew proof paint. So, if you're interested in saving money *and* solving
your mildew problem, dial the number below.
It'll connect you to everything you need plus a lower price.

775-1466

Coatings for every surface from the most knowledgeable and service oriented paint people.
AT THE TOP OF RAPHUNE HILL, ST. THOMAS, VIRGIN ISLANDS. 775-1466

**CHANGING OUR NAME
COMPLETELY.**

In this example, we substituted the
word 'paint' with other words.

WE HAVE BENJAMIN MOORE PAINT.
WE HAVE MARTIN SENOUR PAINT.
WE HAVE VULKEM AND TOUGHKOTE ROOF COATINGS.
WE HAVE ALL THE PAINT SUNDRIES.
WE HAVE LOW PRICES.

SO IF YOU HAVE TO PAINT SOMETHING, WE HAVE EVERYTHING.

THE 'HAVE' DEPOT

Coatings for every surface from the most knowledgeable and service oriented paint people.
AT THE TOP OF RAPHUNE HILL, ST. THOMAS, VIRGIN ISLANDS. 775-1466

LOOKING FOR PURDY PROFESSIONAL PAINT BRUSHES? GOT IT!
LOOKING FOR VULKEM ROOF COATINGS? GOT IT!
LOOKING FOR SUPERLATIVE PAINT COLOR MATCHING? GOT IT!
LOOKING FOR BENJAMIN MOORE PAINT? GOT IT!

IF IT HAS ANYTHING TO DO WITH PAINT,
WE GOT IT!

THE 'GOT IT' DEPOT

Coatings for every surface from the most knowledgeable and service oriented paint people.
AT THE TOP OF RAPHUNE HILL, ST. THOMAS, VIRGIN ISLANDS. 775-1466

WE BE GOOD.
WE BE FAST.
WE BE FRIENDLY.
WE BE WELL STOCKED.

SO IF YOU NEED PAINT,
YOU KNOW WHERE TO BE.

THE 'BE' DEPOT

Coatings for every surface from the most knowledgeable and service oriented paint people.
AT THE TOP OF RAPHUNE HILL, ST. THOMAS, VIRGIN ISLANDS. 775-1466

WE ARE FAST.
WE ARE INEXPENSIVE.
WE ARE WELL STOCKED.
AND WE ARE VERY FRIENDLY.

SO IF YOU NEED PAINT,
YOU KNOW WHERE WE ARE.

THE 'ARE' DEPOT

Coatings for every surface from the most knowledgeable and service oriented paint people.
AT THE TOP OF RAPHUNE HILL, ST. THOMAS, VIRGIN ISLANDS. 775-1466

> *"My fellow constituents!
> If you donate $17.96 to my election
> campaign, I'll give you a free gallon of
> my MoorCraft interior latex semi-gloss
> paint in any pastel color shade you want.
> Just come to my campaign headquarters
> located in The Paint Depot."*

VOTE FOR
BENJAMIN MOORE
COMMISSIONER OF PAINT

Paid for by the Benjamin Moore election
committee headquartered at
The Paint Depot, St. Thomas, V.I. 775-1466

COMMISSIONER OF PAINT AD CAMPAIGN.

This campaign was written to tie into the local election. Before the Benjamin Moore paint line was acquired, we ran headlines that had Re-elect Martin Senour for Paint Commissioner. When we added the Benjamin Moore paint line, I thought we'd run a campaign against each of our paint line brands.

The ads ran the same way in the newspaper. One ad ran on the left hand page and the other ad on the right hand page. All the ads ran on three consecutive page spreads in the newspaper.

At the end, you'll read how one 'candidate' challenges the other to a debate in a future edition of the newspaper.

The full page you'll see later is the 'debate' ad.

Not shown here were the 3' x 4' election posters we had printed up (Vote for Benjamin Moore, Commissioner of Paint) which were placed among the actual election posters for senate and governor candidates.

"Is that all my opponent Benjamin Moore can offer you? I can do much better! If you donate $14.78 to my election campaign, which by way, is $3.18 less, I'll give you a free gallon of my Proline Premium interior latex semi-gloss paint in any pastel color shade you want. So how do you like that!"

VOTE FOR

MARTIN SENOUR

COMMISSIONER OF PAINT

Paid for by the Martin Senour election committee headquartered at The Paint Depot, St. Thomas, V.I. 775-1466

"It seems my opponent, Martin Senour, thinks he'll be a better paint commissioner. Well, let me tell you something. I'll be a much more colorful representative. Plus, I have the endorsement of more interior designers. So there! What do you have to say to that!"

VOTE FOR

BENJAMIN MOORE
COMMISSIONER OF PAINT

Paid for by the Benjamin Moore election committee headquartered at The Paint Depot, St. Thomas, V.I. 775-1466

"My opponent, Mr. Benjamin Moore thinks he's a better candidate because he's more colorful. Well, here is an important fact: my interior latex semi-gloss paint costs less than his interior latex semi-gloss paint. He might be more colorful, but I'll be more fiscally responsible. So, Mr. Benjamin Moore, how will you answer that?"

VOTE FOR

MARTIN SENOUR

COMMISSIONER OF PAINT

Paid for by the Martin Senour election committee headquartered at The Paint Depot, St. Thomas, V.I. 775-1466

"You want to talk price! Well, my honorable opponent, my paints may cost a little bit more, but I've got more solid content in my high end paints than you or any one else on island!
You get what you pay for. I've got integrity and quality running in my blood.
We'll let the voters decide!"

VOTE FOR
BENJAMIN MOORE
COMMISSIONER OF PAINT

Paid for by the Benjamin Moore election committee headquartered at
The Paint Depot, St. Thomas, V.I. 775-1466

"WHAT!? You dare to impugn my quality!! Then I challenge you to a debate in this newspaper on Thursday September 7 on page 7! And bring your paint brush!"

VOTE FOR

MARTIN SENOUR
COMMISSIONER OF PAINT

Paid for by the Martin Senour election committee headquartered at The Paint Depot, St. Thomas, V.I. 775-1466

COMMISSIONER OF PAINT DEBATE!

Between
Martin Senour and Benjamin Moore

(Sponsored by The League of Virgin Island Painters)

QUESTION:
If you were painting a lobbyist's lobby, what would you use?

Martin Senour:
I would use a real nice green color, like the green you see on the back of a US dollar. This would make the lobby rich looking.

Benjamin Moore:
I agree with Martin Senour on the color. But I would recommend that the paint be washable.

QUESTION:
If someone called you to paint the town red, which shade would you use?

Martin Senour:
I'd use Proline Supreme exterior latex semi-gloss and choose "red wagon" as the shade of red.

Benjamin Moore:
For me, I'd use my Super Spec interior latex semi-gloss and for the color, I'd pick "tricycle red".

QUESTION:
Please complete the following: If elected Commissioner of Paint I promise to...

Martin Senour:
I promise to continue delivering the lowest prices and great quality paint. I also pledge that my staff will be there six days a week to answer any paint questions.

Benjamin Moore:
If elected Commissioner of Paint, I promise to always have the most exciting colors available. I also promise the best quality representation for your walls.

We encourage all voters to go to The Paint Depot and buy either Benjamin Moore or Martin Senour paint. We will tally total gallons purchased by makers between today and November 7 and decide who will be the Commissioner of Paint for the next term.
Vote often!

THE PAINT DEPOT

Coatings for every surface from the most knowledgeable and service oriented paint people.
AT THE TOP OF RAPHUNE HILL, ST. THOMAS, VIRGIN ISLANDS. 775-1466

Y2K COMPLIANT.

Sometimes an event happens just once, like January 1, 2000. There was such a fuss about what might happen to the world on Y2K. This ad takes advantage of that event. We ran it in the last week of December 1999.

Y2K PAINT NOTICE!

Please be advised that all Martin-Senour paints are Y2K compliant.
This means that our paints won't fall off your walls when January 1, 2000 arrives.

THE PAINT DEPOT

Coatings for every surface from the most knowledgeable and service oriented paint people.
AT THE TOP OF RAPHUNE HILL, ST. THOMAS, VIRGIN ISLANDS. 775-1466

OUR CHRISTMAS CARDS WILL BE MAILED VERY EARLY THIS YEAR.

Postage stamps are going up .02 cents on May 14th.
So, we decided to mail our Christmas cards now to save money.
I know, .02 cents doesn't sound like much, but look at how
being frugal helps you:

We priced out 3" bristle paint brushes
at three different places. ($1.49, $1.37 and $1.07).
Guess who sells it for $1.07? That's right, us.

You can buy a gallon of Zinsser 123 primer for $31.99, $24.69 or $21.56 in
the Virgin Islands. If you guessed we sell that same gallon for $21.56,
then Christmas is coming early for you.

A gallon of paint thinner fetches $10.95 and $8.26 elsewhere.
We sell it for $6.75.

We could go on and on but if we don't hurry and
get those Christmas cards out, we'll miss the mailing deadline!

THE PAINT DEPOT

Coatings for every surface from the most knowledgeable and service oriented paint people.
AT THE TOP OF RAPHUNE HILL, ST. THOMAS, VIRGIN ISLANDS. 775-1466

YES, WE ACTUALLY MAILED OUR CHRISTMAS CARDS IN MAY.

Prior to 2007, there was no Forever stamps. People would have to buy .02 cent stamps to add to their old stamps on the envelope in order to meet the new postage rate.

The postage rate increase was always news. So, in order to save ourselves .02 cents, we decided to mail our Christmas cards in May of that year and tie that in as to why we have the best prices.

The actual Christmas card that was mailed had most of the copy from this ad.

ONE OF THE FEW ADS WE RAN WITH A VISUAL.

I called the Martin Senour paint tech department to make sure that this paint really had the highest solids per gallon. I then double checked that we truly had the lowest price anywhere because I didn't want to eat a full page newsprint ad.

Martin Senour liked the copy and said they'd cover 50% of the ad cost if we put a picture on the product on. Seemed like a good deal to me.

"IF YOU CAN FIND A BETTER QUALITY PAINT AT A LOWER REGULAR PRICE I'LL EAT THIS AD!"

Michael Perron

We're taking our very best paint, Platinum interior, Platinum exterior and putting them on sale at prices *never* before seen. Martin-Senour's Platinum paints have more solids, more guts, more quality ingredients than just about anything else on the market. We want you to try this super high quality paint and to do that, we'll give it to you at a price, that no one can beat! Or I'll eat these words!

PLATINUM EXTERIOR LATEX SATIN, WHITE AND PASTEL
5 gal. reg. $149.00
NOW $79.30*, SAVE 47%!
1 gal. reg. $31.50
NOW $17.05*, SAVE 47%

PLATINUM INTERIOR LATEX EGGSHELL, WHITE AND PASTEL
5 gal reg. $136.50
NOW $70.55*, SAVE 48%
1 gal. reg. $27.95
NOW $14.57*, SAVE 48%!

*Sale price shows 30% off regular price plus a $5.00 per gallon manufacturer mail-in rebate. Rebate portion is limited to 10 gallons per household and mailing address. Purchases for rebate must be made between May 12 and July 5, 2004. Official redemption forms are available at The Paint Depot. See us for complete details.

THE PAINT DEPOT
GREAT PRODUCTS, INCREDIBLE SERVICE AND LOW PRICES.
AL COHEN PLAZA, ST. THOMAS, VIRGIN ISLANDS. 775-1466

HOW MANY WAYS CAN YOU SAY "WE'RE HAVING A SALE!"

Yes, we run sale ads. Surprisingly, our competitors seldom had paint sales. I remember one day running into one of them and he asked me "Why are you discounting your paint in December when people are buying it anyways to freshen up for the holidays? You don't have to put it on sale now."

We had a lot of sales in the early years of our business and we used them to buy market share.

It costs money to acquire a new customer. But once you have them and take really good care of them, they are with you for a very, very long time.

AMBIDEXTROUS SALE!

If you want to save money left and right, you need to come to our "ambidextrous sale".
One one hand, all Martin-Senour paints are on sale from 20% to 50% off.
On the other hand, all paint accessories are discounted by 10% to 35%.
But you'll need to hurry. Sale ends July 5, 2004.
That's right, there's only one week left!

THE PAINT DEPOT

Coatings for every surface from the most knowledgeable and service oriented paint people.
AT THE TOP OF RAPHUNE HILL, ST. THOMAS, VIRGIN ISLANDS. 775-1466

**RUNNING A SALE
DURING
TAX SEASON.**

This sale ad ran six times a few weeks prior to April 15th, tax day.

I was particularly happy with the last line.

IT'S LIKE NOT PAYING YOUR INCOME TAX!

The average income tax rate for a
Virgin Islander is about 18%.
So that's what we decided to discount all
Martin-Senour paints in the month of April.
Are you in the 20% tax bracket? We'll give you 20% off
Great Life exterior latex paints.
Make even more money and are paying 30% tax?
No problem. We'llgive you 30% off our ProLine
Premium interior latex semi-gloss
enamel, white and pastel colors.
And if you don't pay any tax at all,
then you must be very, very rich
and we can't give you a discount.
Sorry.

THE PAINT DEPOT

Coatings for every surface from the most knowledgeable and service oriented paint people.
AT THE TOP OF RAPHUNE HILL, ST. THOMAS, VIRGIN ISLANDS. 775-1466

COATINGS FOR EVERY SURFACE.

We carried coatings for every surface. In addition to boat paint, we have cistern coatings, roof coatings, car paints, industrial coatings and of course, house paint.

TITANIC SALE ON BOAT PAINT!

AWLGRIP: all in stock colors on sale, example, Matterhorn white, 1 gallon regular $165.00, NOW $137.74
PETIT TRINIDAD: antifouling paint, 75% copper, 1 gallon regular $165.00, NOW $136.95
PETIT ACP: ablative antifouling paint, 1 gallon regular $159.00, NOW $131.97

THE PAINT DEPOT

Coatings for every surface from the most knowledgeable and service oriented paint people.
AT THE TOP OF RAPHUNE HILL, ST. THOMAS, VIRGIN ISLANDS. 775-1466

HOW DO YOU SAY 'ON SALE'.

There are so many ways of saying your prices are better. Here's a selection of them.

WHY IS 20% OFF AT THE PAINT DEPOT BETTER THAN 20% OFF ELSEWHERE?

(Because our prices are lower to begin with!)

THE PAINT DEPOT

Coatings for every surface from the most knowledgeable and service oriented paint people.
AT THE TOP OF RAPHUNE HILL, ST. THOMAS, VIRGIN ISLANDS. 775-1466

GO FIGURE!

If you take 30% off the price of any Martin-Senour paint, then get an additional $5.00 back for every gallon* you buy on top of that, what would you get?
The best price ever, that's what!

*Offer ends July 5, 2004. Rebate is limited to 10 gallons per household. Get $5.00 rebate per gallon on Platinum paint, maximum $50.00, and $3.00 per gallon on Great Life or Great Outdoor stains, maximum $30.00. See us for complete details.

THE PAINT DEPOT

Coatings for every surface from the most knowledgeable and service oriented paint people.
AT THE TOP OF RAPHUNE HILL, ST. THOMAS, VIRGIN ISLANDS. 775-1466

ONLY 7 DAYS LEFT? THAT'S RIGHT!

Only 7 days left to save 20% to 50% on ALL Martin Senour paints
and 10% to 40% on ALL paint accessories.
So come on in. If you're heading in from the east, turn left, from the west, turn right. But do it right now!

THE PAINT DEPOT

Coatings for every surface from the most knowledgeable and service oriented paint people.
AT THE TOP OF RAPHUNE HILL, ST. THOMAS, VIRGIN ISLANDS. 775-1466

Everyone complains about the price of gas. We ran this ad in 2007 when a gallon of gas cost $3.40 here in St. Thomas.

A GALLON OF GAS FOP ONLY $1.34!

That was the price back in 1995. Back then, our water-based roof coating retailed for $119. for 5 gallons. Twelve years later, you can buy 5 gallons of our ToughKote NSF approved water based roof coating for $119. But, this can't last forever. Prices have to go up. (But not quite yet.) In other words, hurry over! Because if ever there was a time to recoat your roof, this is it! By the way, our roof coating price is $48.40 LESS PER BUCKET than the other leading brand sold on island. I gotta say it again. Our ToughKote roof coating WILL SAVE YOU $48.40 PER BUCKET versus the other popular brand. Now, isn't driving here for your roof coating 'gas money' well spent?

THE PAINT DEPOT

Coatings for every surface from the most knowledgeable and service oriented paint people.

AT THE TOP OF RAPHUNE HILL, ST. THOMAS, VIRGIN ISLANDS. 775-1466

"I ONLY WANT HALF YOUR MONEY!"

The regular price for a five gallon pail of Martin-Senour's Proline Supreme Interior antique white, semi-gloss paint is $99.95. But, as I said, I only want half of that or $49.97. It's only available in 5 gallon pails and I'm only putting 300 gallons on sale at this incredible price.
Should I have to tell you to hurry?

THE PAINT DEPOT

Coatings for every surface from the most knowledgeable and service oriented paint people.
AT THE TOP OF RAPHUNE HILL, ST. THOMAS, VIRGIN ISLANDS. 775-1466

Sometimes you don't even need a
headline.

Just checking to make sure you're reading these ads. And if you are, then this is your lucky day
because we are taking our Martin-Senour Proline Supreme interior latex semi-gloss,
antique white paint, regular $99.95 for 5 gallons, and putting it on sale at 50% off!
You read right, that's half price or $49.97! Now here comes the fine print.
It's only available in 5 gallon pails, and I'm only putting 300 gallons on sale at this price.
Should I have to tell you to hurry?

THE PAINT DEPOT

Coatings for every surface from the most knowledgeable and service oriented paint people.
AT THE TOP OF RAPHUNE HILL, ST. THOMAS, VIRGIN ISLANDS. 775-1466

VISUAL REINFORCEMENT.

It's not often we strayed from all copy ads. But this was a good visual.

YOUR CHECK
IS IN THE MAIL.

When you buy any Platinum Interior or Exterior, Great Life exterior paint or Great Outdoor stain, you'll not only get 20% off the price, you'll also be eligible to receive a rebate check for up to $75.00 off your purchase price!

(Offer ends July 6, 2003. Rebate is limited to 15 gallons per household. Get $5.00 rebate per gallon on Platinum paint, maximum $75.00, and $3.00 per gallon rebate on Great Life or Great Outdoor, maximum $45.00. See us for complete details.)

THE PAINT DEPOT

Coatings for every surface from the most knowledgeable and service oriented paint people.

AT THE TOP OF RAPHUNE HILL, ST. THOMAS, VIRGIN ISLANDS. 775-1466

PSSSSST! HEY, ARE YOU LOOKING FOR SOME CHEAP DATES?

Then keep November 15 to December 21, 2005 open
because everything in the store goes on sale.
We might be cheap, but we're real good.

THE PAINT DEPOT

Coatings for every surface from the most knowledgeable and service oriented paint people.
AT THE TOP OF RAPHUNE HILL, ST. THOMAS, VIRGIN ISLANDS. 775-1466

CHEAP THRILLS

I DON'T KNOW ABOUT YOU, BUT CHEAP PRICES ARE ALWAYS A THRILL TO ME. SO, WITHOUT TEASING YOU FURTHER, HERE ARE SOME SUPER HOT, THRILLING, CHEAP PRICES.

ToughKote roof coating, white, 5 gallons reg. $119.95
NOW $95.96 SAVE 20%!
(Oh baby, yes!)
Proline Premium interior latex s-g, white & pastel colors, 5 gallons reg. $88.75
NOW $62.13 SAVE 30%!
(Don't stop!)
Stretchcoat Acrylic Masonry Primer, 5 gallons reg. $104.00
NOW $78.00 SAVE 25%!
(Keep that cheap talk coming!)
Proline Premium Int/Ext latex flat, white and pastel colors, 5 gallons reg. $69.95
NOW $45.47 SAVE 35%!
(I bet you say that to all your customers!)
Proline Premium Ext. latex s-g, white & pastel colors, 5 gallons reg. $94.95
NOW $71.21 SAVE $25%!
(Yes! Yes! Yes!)
Martin-Senour Int/Ext Marine Spar Varnish, 1 gallon reg. $34.95
NOW 26.21 SAVE 25%!
(Give me more!!!)
O.K., LET'S MAKE IT $22.72 A GALLON. THAT'S 35% OFF!
(You know that I'll still love you after the sale.)

THE PAINT DEPOT

Coatings for every surface from the most knowledgeable and service oriented paint people.
AT THE TOP OF RAPHUNE HILL, ST. THOMAS, VIRGIN ISLANDS. 775-1466

WINTER COAT SALE!

If you're looking to put a new coat on your roof this winter, then now is the time to do it.
We're putting our ToughKote elastomeric roof coating on sale!
Five gallons of ToughKote white or pastel color finish coat was $119.95, NOW $98.36!
But hurry, sales ends soon!

THE PAINT DEPOT

Coatings for every surface from the most knowledgeable and service oriented paint people.
AT THE TOP OF RAPHUNE HILL, ST. THOMAS, VIRGIN ISLANDS. 775-1466

GIVEAWAYS.

We also had sales where we'd give-away something. Here's one where you got 20% off and a free T-shirt.

So, what makes an ad a great ad? It makes money!

"GET 20% OFF *AND* TAKE THE SHIRT OFF MY BACK!"

When you buy 10 gallons or more of Martin-Senour paints between now and the end of September, you'll not only get 20% off the price, but I'll give you the shirt off my back! Of course, if you'd rather have a brand new T-shirt instead of the one I'm actually wearing, that's OK too.
(Limit one Paint Depot T-shirt per customer per day. Offer ends September 30.)

THE PAINT DEPOT

Coatings for every surface from the most knowledgeable and service oriented paint people.
AT THE TOP OF RAPHUNE HILL, ST. THOMAS, VIRGIN ISLANDS. 775-1466

The month of December is a big month for paint sales. People are freshening up their homes for the holidays.

ALL I WANT
FOR CHRISTMAS IS...

...30% off all Martin-Senour paints. And 50% off all Ralph Lauren paints. Let's see, I also want 20% off all ToughKote roof coating. And how about 30% off all those professional Purdy paint brushes. And while you're at it, can I have a free, bright red, empty 5 gallon bucket so I can stick my Christmas tree in?

(The answer is yes to everything except the 5 gallon bucket. You'll have to spend $50.00 or more to get that for free. Sale ends December 22, 2001. Cash sales only. Hurry, you don't have many shopping days left until Christmas.)

THE PAINT DEPOT

Coatings for every surface from the most knowledgeable and service oriented paint people. AT THE TOP OF RAPHUNE HILL, ST. THOMAS, VIRGIN ISLANDS. 775-1466

FREE LOTTERY TICKETS.

Who hasn't purchased a lottery ticket, even once. Here we make every lottery loser a winner in two ways. A nice discount on paint and a replacement lottery ticket for your losing ticket.

LOTTERY LOSERS!

Your luck has changed.
Bring in any used lottery ticket and we'll make you a winner in two ways. First, we'll take 20% off any Martin-Senour paint. Second, we'll trade in your old lottery ticket for one new Powerball ticket with your purchase of two gallons or more. Who knows, you just might win enough money to buy paint for every single house in the Virgin Islands.

(Offer ends May 31, 2003. Limit one free Powerball ticket per customer per day with purchase of minimum two gallons of Martin-Senour paint.)

THE PAINT DEPOT

Coatings for every surface from the most knowledgeable and service oriented paint people.
AT THE TOP OF RAPHUNE HILL, ST. THOMAS, VIRGIN ISLANDS. 775-1466

I'm no longer on social media, but when Twitter first came out, I loved the limit of 140 characters. This is what copywriting is about. To make very word count.

THE WINNING NUMBERS ARE... 7..75..14..66

Hey! That's The Paint Depot's phone number!
That's right. And we're going to make you a winner in two ways.
First, bring in any used lottery ticket and we'll
take 20% off any Martin-Senour paint. Second, we'll trade in your old ticket
for one brand new Powerball ticket with your purchase of two gallons or more.
Who knows, you just might win 'the big one' and have enough money
to buy paint for every single house in the Virgin Islands.

(Offer ends May 31, 2003. Limit one free Powerball ticket per
customer per day with purchase of minimum
two gallons of Martin-Senour paint.)

THE PAINT DEPOT
Coatings for every surface from the most knowledgeable and service oriented paint people.
AT THE TOP OF RAPHUNE HILL, ST. THOMAS, VIRGIN ISLANDS. 775-1466

OUR BEST SALE PROMOTION. EVER.

We've had lots of sales but this particular one resulted in our highest monthly sales at that time. We put together 2,000 prizes from key chains to T-shirts to toaster ovens. We had a storewide sale as well.

You'd come in, buy paint and we'd give you a fortune cookie. Open it up and you'd win something. Might be small, might be big but everybody won something.

In addition to the print ads, we did TV, radio plus a 4-color, 8 page glossy direct mail flyer that went to every St. Thomas resident.

PAINT YOUR WAY TO A SMALL FORTUNE!

Literally!
With your purchase of paint, you get a small fortune...a fortune cookie that is. Crumble it open and you automatically win a prize.
Could be a toaster oven, T-shirt, tote bag, radio, keyring or other neat prize.
But there's more! (There always is.) Everything in the store is on sale from 10% to 50% off!
But hurry, the last cookie crumbles on July 6. Cash sales only.

THE PAINT DEPOT

Coatings for every surface from the most knowledgeable and service oriented paint people.
AT THE TOP OF RAPHUNE HILL, ST. THOMAS, VIRGIN ISLANDS. 775-1466

WHEN THE COOKIE CRUMBLES, YOU WIN!

Literally! With your purchase of paint, you get a free fortune cookie. Crumble it open and you automatically win a prize! Could be a toaster oven, t-shirt, calculator, radio, key ring or other neat prize. But there's more! (There always is.) Everything in the store is on sale from 10% to 50% off! Platinum paint, 35% off, Great Life paint, 30% off, ToughKote roof coating, 20% off, Ralph Lauren paint (limited supplies) 50% off! But hurry, the last cookie crumbles on July 6th, 2002. Cash sales only.

THE PAINT DEPOT

Coatings for every surface from the most knowledgeable and service oriented paint people.
AT THE TOP OF RAPHUNE HILL, ST. THOMAS, VIRGIN ISLANDS. 775-1466

ネユメメル。 ネユヌナ ミチノホヤ モチフナ。

TRANSLATION: Save a fortune on paint!

With your purchase of paint, you get a free fortune cookie. Open it and you win instantly! Could be a toaster oven, t-shirt, tote bag, radio, key ring or other neat prize. But there's more! (There always is.) Everything in the store is on sale from 10% to 50% off! Platinum paint, 35% off, Great Life 30% off, ToughKote roof coating, 20% off, Ralph Lauren paint (limited supplies) 50% off! But hurry, the last cookie crumbles on July 6, 2002. Cash only sales.

THE PAINT DEPOT

COATINGS FOR EVERY SURFACE FROM THE MOST KNOWLEDGEABLE AND SERVICE ORIENTED PAINT PEOPLE.
AL COHEN PLAZA, ST. THOMAS, VIRGIN ISLANDS. 775-1466

WIN A SMALL FORTUNE WITH EVERY PAINT PURCHASE!

Actually, it's a fortune cookie. But hey, every cookie has a small fortune inside. Could be a free T-shirt, key chain, toaster oven, watch, calculator, radio, who knows. You get a fortune cookie with your purchase of paint and every fortune cookie is a winner. But here comes the best part, everything in the store is on sale from 10% to 50% off! Platinum paint, 35% off, Great Life paint, 30% off, Ralph Lauren paint (limited supplies), 50% off. With savings like this, you'll save a small fortune as well.

(Sale ends July 6. Cash sales only.)

THE PAINT DEPOT

Coatings for every surface from the most knowledgeable and service oriented paint people.
AT THE TOP OF RAPHUNE HILL, ST. THOMAS, VIRGIN ISLANDS. 775-1466

THE *OTHER* CANNES FILM FESTIVAL.

We tied the Cannes Film Festival with a paint sale and free tickets to the local movie theater or a free video rental.

THE CANS FILM FESTIVAL

Buy two gallon cans of any Martin-Senour paint and get either a free ticket to the movies or two video rentals from Island Video.
If you're looking for a great film, Martin-Senour is the paint to get. The toughest, most beautiful paint film around.
So, the more paint film you put on your walls, the movie films you get to see. Hey, this may not be quite
like the Cannes Film Festival in France, but we think it's pretty close.
(Cash sales only. Offer ends December 23, 2000. Free movie ticket applies to any film showing at Market Square East or Cinema One in St. Thomas; free movie
rental applies to a two day film rental at any Island Video location.)

THE PAINT DEPOT
Coatings for every surface from the most knowledgeable and service oriented paint people.
AT THE TOP OF RAPHUNE HILL, ST. THOMAS, VIRGIN ISLANDS. 775-1466

YOUR TICKET TO A GREAT FILM!

If you're looking for a great film, Martin Senour is the best paint to get. The toughest, most beautiful paint film around.
And until December 23, 2000, you get a choice of either a free ticket to the movies or two video rentals from Island Video
when you buy two gallon cans of any Martin Senour paint. So, the more paint film you put on your walls,
the more movie films you get to see.
(Cash sales only. Offer ends December 23, 2000. Free movie ticket applies to any film showing at Market Square East or Cinema One in St. Thomas; free movie
rental applies to a two day film rental at any Island Video location.)

THE PAINT DEPOT

Coatings for every surface from the most knowledgeable and service oriented paint people.
AT THE TOP OF RAPHUNE HILL, ST. THOMAS, VIRGIN ISLANDS. 775-1466

FREE PAINT BUCKETS.

We were giving away free empty paint buckets. Ours were all red with The Paint Depot name on it. Because everybody can use an empty 5 gallon bucket at home, this promotion was very well received.

FREE SHOPPING BAG!
(BUT HEY, NOT JUST *ANY* SHOPPING BAG.)

With your purchase of $25.00 or more, you get to keep your shopping bag, in this case, a heavy-duty, 5 gallon empty plastic bucket.
Which makes everyone else's bag 'pail' by comparison. Need another reason to shop?
How about 10% to 50% off everything in the store! Like all Martin-Senour paint, 30% off;
all Ralph Lauren paint, 50% off; Vulkem 931 sealant, 25% offf.
Limit one pail per customer or while supplies last, so hurry, hurry!

THE PAINT DEPOT
Coatings for every surface from the most knowledgeable and service oriented paint people.
AT THE TOP OF RAPHUNE HILL, ST. THOMAS, VIRGIN ISLANDS. 775-1466

5 GALLONS OF FREE AIR WITH EVERY $25. PURCHASE!

With every purchase of $25.00 or more this week, we'll give you 5 gallons of free air.
Now, you're probably wondering how you'll take your 5 gallons of air home with you. We'll, our air comes packaged in a beautiful, red plastic five gallon empty bucket. There's no lid, so don't spill any on the way out.

(Free 5 gallon, empty paint bucket with the purchase of $25.00 or more. Limit one per day per customer.)

THE PAINT DEPOT

Coatings for every surface from the most knowledgeable and service oriented paint people.
AT THE TOP OF RAPHUNE HILL, ST. THOMAS, VIRGIN ISLANDS. 775-1466

HOW WE ADVERTISED OUR GIVEAWAY CALENDARS.

Benjamin Moore produced calendars as giveaways one year. They consisted of twelve different pictures of dogs in designer dog houses which were painted with Benjamin Moore paint.

So, gotta find a way to make people want them.

Remember, if you can make people gasp when they read the headline, that's good.

FREE NUDE CALENDARS!

With any purchase of $1.00 or more, we'll give you a free 2006, full color, nude calendar! It's a calendar of designer dog houses and yes, the dogs that are modeling in it have no clothes on, which qualifies them as nude. Hey, we wouldn't want to be accused of misleading advertising. Oh, and the dog houses are all painted with Benjamin Moore paint. Gotta sell something here too.

THE PAINT DEPOT

Coatings for every surface from the most knowledgeable and service oriented paint people.
AT THE TOP OF RAPHUNE HILL, ST. THOMAS, VIRGIN ISLANDS. 775-1466

TRICK OR TREAT?

Get both right here. We can help you with all kinds of paint tricks. Like how to achieve a virtual brush mark free painting by using Penetrol or Floetrol in the paint. And with every purchase, you get a treat...a free designer dog house calendar. (They're really nice!)

THE PAINT DEPOT

Coatings for every surface from the most knowledgeable and service oriented paint people.

AT THE TOP OF RAPHUNE HILL, ST. THOMAS, VIRGIN ISLANDS. 775-1466

HOME DEPOT WERE GOING TO MOVE DOWN THE ROAD FROM US.

As soon as we got a whiff that Home Depot were going to open one of their big boxes virtually across the street from us, we got busy.

The first thng we did was call a number of paint retailers located very close to Home Depots in the U.S. They said to 'give great service and you'll survive'. But survival is not what we wanted to do. We wanted to thrive!

While Home Depot was being constructed, we visited their closest outlet in San Juan, Puerto Rico. We purchased a variety of paint and paint sundries and had them shipped to our store. We then produced TV commercials and print ads.

I did the TV spots myself. I purchased a camcorder, mounted it on a tripod in front of our store and stood in front with both their product and ours and read the print ads verbatim, with a special emphasis on the word "OR".

Because people perceive that Home Depot had lower prices, we needed to refute that claim. Perceptions can be nothing more than rumors. But you need to crush them.

Results: when Home Depot opened in 2003, people went and compared prices to ours. Our business not only survived, we increased sales by 10% over the next 12 months after they opened.

Recently, I went back and compared our sales and profit numbers from 2003 when Home Depot opened and today in 2023.

In that time, our sales increased 83% and our profit increased 376%. Home Depot is still there. And so are we.

AN AD IS A PROMISE.

The bigger the promise, the better the ad. Are you saving them money? time? better service? Then you need to quantify your promise.

I can't tell you how many times I've seen the line 'you've tried the rest, now try the best'. It means nothing. No one will believe you. As a matter of fact, you've probably turned off prospective customers.

If you want to say you have lower prices, you need to quantify, to prove it.

If you can't prove it, why would the reader believe you?

You can buy 5 gallons of better quality exterior s/g paint (Glidden) at **HOME DEPOT in Puerto Rico** for $89.67

OR

You can buy 5 gallons of better quality exterior s/g paint (Proline Supreme) at **THE PAINT DEPOT in St. Thomas** <u>for $84.95 and save $4.72!</u>

SURPRISED?

You shouldn't be.
We've always had great products, incredible service *and* low prices.

THE PAINT DEPOT

Coatings for every surface from the most knowledgeable and service oriented paint people.
AT THE TOP OF RAPHUNE HILL, ST. THOMAS, VIRGIN ISLANDS. 775-1466

You can buy a 10.1 ounce tube of GE clear, 100% silicone sealant at **HOME DEPOT in Puerto Rico** for $4.58

OR

You can buy a 10.1 ounce tube of DAP clear, 100% silicone sealant at **THE PAINT DEPOT in St. Thomas <u>for $4.37 and save $0.21!</u>**

SURPRISED?
You shouldn't be.
We've always had great products,
incredible service *and* low prices.

THE PAINT DEPOT
Coatings for every surface from the most knowledgeable and service oriented paint people.
AT THE TOP OF RAPHUNE HILL, ST. THOMAS, VIRGIN ISLANDS. 775-1466

You can buy 5 gallons of better quality exterior s/g paint (Glidden) at **HOME DEPOT in Puerto Rico** for $89.67

You can buy 5 gallons of better quality exterior s/g paint (Proline Supreme) at **THE PAINT DEPOT in St. Thomas <u>for $84.95 and save $4.72!</u>**

SURPRISED?
You shouldn't be.
We've always had great products, incredible service *and* low prices.

THE PAINT DEPOT

Coatings for every surface from the most knowledgeable and service oriented paint people.
AT THE TOP OF RAPHUNE HILL, ST. THOMAS, VIRGIN ISLANDS. 775-1466

MINE IS BIGGER!

You know *exactly* what I'm talking about...
the size of my paint inventory, of course!

Because if you needed enough Martin-Senour Proline Premium interior
latex semi-gloss to paint 100,000 sq. ft. of walls and you called at 7:30 this
morning, we could mix it up to the color your want and have it ready
for you before lunch time. And you'd pay only $62.13
per pail, a 30% savings!

Or how about enough Vulkem roof coating to do a
30,000 sq. ft. roof? It's in stock, right now. And it's on sale.

Last month, someone needed 500 lbs of rags.
No problem, we had it in stock.

Need a special primer? Some places carry five different primers,
others a dozen or so. Not us.
We've got 43, (let me spell that out, *forty-three*) different primers.
That means we've got every surface primed and covered
better than anyone else.

So besides great products, incredible service and
low prices, we can now say we're bigger
where it really counts.

THE PAINT DEPOT

Coatings for every surface from the most knowledgeable and service oriented paint people.
AT THE TOP OF RAPHUNE HILL, ST. THOMAS, VIRGIN ISLANDS. 775-1466

CRUSH WRONG PERCEPTIONS.

Some people assumed that because Home Depot is so big, they must have more of everything. We ran this ad to counter this misperception.

DON'T BE AFRAID!

We ran this ad after Home Depot had already opened across the street. We were not afraid of comparing their prices to ours. The headline is local slang.

"ME NO 'FRAID!"

When it comes to great products, incredible service AND low prices, we're not afraid of comparison to anybody on island, *anybody*! For example, right now you can buy 5 gallons of Proline Premium interior latex semi-gloss paint for $62.13, that's a 30% saving! And what about painting accessories. A 3 inch white china bristle brush sells for $2.47 at that big box across the street from us. We sell the same brush for $1.07! That's right, two brushes from us costs less than one from 'them'. Or, how about a quality 9" roller frame. It's $4.57 'there' and only $2.66 'here'. This is just an itsy, bitsy part of our storewide sale. So don't be afraid to come in and save up to 48%.

THE PAINT DEPOT

Coatings for every surface from the most knowledgeable and service oriented paint people.

AT THE TOP OF RAPHUNE HILL, ST. THOMAS, VIRGIN ISLANDS. 775-1466

WE GO THE EXTRA 5,290 FEET.

I *know* there's only 5,280 feet in a mile,
but we like to go that all important extra ten feet.
Why? Because if you have trouble with a leaky roof, we'll
go to your home (even if it is more than a mile away), and
when we get there, we'll climb those ten feet to get up on
your roof to check it out personally.
We can usually resolve most paint or roof coating
problems on the phone. But if we can't, we'll go
the extra mile, plus the ten feet.
In other words, the whole nine yards.

THE PAINT DEPOT

Coatings for every surface from the most knowledgeable and service oriented paint people.
AT THE TOP OF RAPHUNE HILL, ST. THOMAS, VIRGIN ISLANDS. 775-1466

CUSTOMER SERVICE. BUT NOT JUST ANY CUSTOMER SERVICE.

The people who buy our paint come in every color, every walk of life, every economic segment.

Governors, senators, paint contractors, rich, not so rich, literally a complete cross section of the population come into our store. Then they all become one thing, a customer.

Everybody gets The Paint Depot experience. Some stores will have one person help with the paint color, it then gets handed off to someone who mixes the color, then you go to a different person to pay for your purchase. And then you carry your purchase out to the car yourself. Here, every employee takes care of the customer from start to finish.

They will help you with the color, the type of paint.

Take you through any paint accessories you might need. They'll mix the paint. Show you the finished color and make sure you're happy. Then they'll add that color to your paint record. Every customer we have has a paint record on file showing the color, formula, their name and what room the color was used in. Then we'll carry your purchase out to your car. Great service is so simple.

Everybody talks about great service. But that needs to be quantified as well. In the ad on the left, we talk about making house calls, something our competitors didn't do.

5,468 YEARS
OF PAINT EXPERIENCE.

You know how some companies like to tell you how many years of experience they have by counting their employees and multiplying by the number of years they worked there? Well, here at The Paint Depot, we like to look at things differently. Our employees have a combined total of 80 fingers. When you think about our huge paint and sundry inventory, it comes in handy to point items out to you. We also have a combined total of 24 lbs of brain matter so when you have a tough paint problem, we can put our collective heads together and find a solution. So, how did we get 5,468 year of paint experience when we've only been in business for 11 years? Well, in every single one of our previous reincarnated lives, we were painters, that's how.

THE PAINT DEPOT

Coatings for every surface from the most knowledgeable and service oriented paint people.
AT THE TOP OF RAPHUNE HILL, ST. THOMAS, VIRGIN ISLANDS. 775-1466

TREAT PEOPLE
LIKE A SOMEBODY.

In this ad, the only product I'm selling is a .90 cent, throwaway paint brush. But what I'm really selling is how we treat people.

WHY YOU SHOULD COME HERE TO BUY A BBQ BASTING BRUSH.

I was in a grocery store the other day and saw a 2" china bristle basting brush for $2.99. We sell those exact same 2" bristle brushes for .90 cents! So, if you're wondering why you would drive all the way here for a .90 cent brush to baste your chicken on the barbecue, other than the fact that you'll save $2.09, I'll tell you. The absolute incredible service. Because even when you're just buying a basting brush, which, coincidentally, can also be used for painting, you'll be treated like a somebody.

THE PAINT DEPOT

Coatings for every surface from the most knowledgeable and service oriented paint people.
AT THE TOP OF RAPHUNE HILL, ST. THOMAS, VIRGIN ISLANDS. 775-1466

EXTRA
EXTRA
EXTRA
EXTRA
EXTRA
LARGE

Shopping at the largest paint store, which we just happen to be, means absolutely nothing. Unless, of course, you are passionate about customer service, which, by the way, we also just happen to be.

This place is still a small, locally owned and operated paint store that just happens to have more experienced paint people (seven of us), more color choices (over 5,000), more inventory and paint accessories than you can shake a paint stick at, plus, much better service than any other place. So, if you're looking for the right paint store size for all your needs, XXXXXL is the perfect fit.

THE PAINT DEPOT

Coatings for every surface from the most knowledgeable and service oriented paint people.
AT THE TOP OF RAPHUNE HILL, ST. THOMAS, VIRGIN ISLANDS. 775-1466

THE "X-FILE"

We only have one name in our "X" file.
But for all the other letters in the alphabet, we have over 8,000 customers on record.

You see, when you choose a custom tinted Martin-Senour paint from us, we create a file with your name, the type of paint used, the color formula, and if you want, even what room you used it in. It's great when you need to order some touch up paint in the future.

And with great products, incredible service and low prices, it's no mystery why we have so many people buy their paint here.

THE PAINT DEPOT

Coatings for every surface from the most knowledgeable and service oriented paint people.
AT THE TOP OF RAPHUNE HILL, ST. THOMAS, VIRGIN ISLANDS. 775-1466

KEEPING CUSTOMER RECORDS.

No one that I know of keeps such detailed customer paint color information. We've been doing it since day one. At last count, we had over 8,000 cards on file.

DETAILED COLOR CARDS INCLUDING A DAB OF EACH COLOR PURCHASED BY OUR CUSTOMERS.

Here is a sample of the color cards we have on every customer. The cards have a dab of the actual color that was mixed.

The top one is of an individual customer. There are an additional two color cards attached to this.

The bottom one is of a hotel. There are an additional 12 cards showing the different buildings, rooms and restaurant colors.

When customers call to order paint, we immediately pull the card and ask what they want. Fool proof, error proof. They get exactly what they want.

Because we've been doing this for 28 years, we often times get a new customer walking in saying they need touch up paint. We ask their name and if we can't find the card, we ask, did you just buy this house? Invariably, they'll say 'yes'. We look up the previous owner, pull the card and then change the card name to the new owner.

I can't tell you how impressed those customers are.

	4/10/08
CLIENT BHandari,Ashu	CONTRACTOR G.P.
PRODUCT; INT OR EXT; SHEEN; BASE; AREA USED IN.	COLOR; FORMULA; SIZE; MIXED BY Bobby
2175-70 275-1B Ceiling living/kitchen	YW-0×3.00 RX-0×2.75 1 gal.
#077 274-4B Walls living/kitchen	YW-0×26.00 BK-0×9.00 OG-11×4.00 WH-1×7.00 1 gal.
#075 274-3B Walls BedRoom/Bath Rm	OY-2×4.00 OG-3×6.00 GY-0×20.00 WH-0×16.00 1 gal.

CLIENT FRENCHMAN COVE - MARKET PLACE GRILL	CONTRACTOR
PRODUCT; INT OR EXT; SHEEN; BASE; AREA USED IN.	COLOR; FORMULA; SIZE; MIXED BY
274-4B	1680
274-4B H.CLUB WARE PT2	2006-20
274-1B H.Club PT3	1115
274-4B H.CLUB Men PT4	1680
274-3B WOMEN PT5	105
276-1B PT6	1114
274-2B PT7	187
274-1B PT8	185

PEOPLE FROM EVERYWHERE.

We are very proud of our employee diversity. We ran this ad during the annual St. Thomas Carnival Festival.

MULTICOLORTURAL

You won't find a more multicolortural place than right here at The Paint Depot. Our staff's ethnic background includes Scotland, Nevis, Poland, Dominica, Quebec, and of course, St. Thomas.
We believe the more colorful your staff, the more colorful your business.
And when your business is paint...mixed paint...colorture, really is, everything.

THE PAINT DEPOT

Coatings for every surface from the most knowledgeable and service oriented paint people.
AT THE TOP OF RAPHUNE HILL, ST. THOMAS, VIRGIN ISLANDS. 775-1466

WHAT'S OUR EMPLOYEE DOING IN YOUR BEDROOM?

Measuring the room to see how much paint will be required and explaining why the paint is peeling on the wall facing your cistern, that's what. We routinely make house calls if we can't solve your problem on the phone.
Got a leak on your roof? We'll climb up and check it out.
Need a recommendation on your outside walls? Call us.
As always, there's no charge for this service.

THE PAINT DEPOT

Coatings for every surface from the most knowledgeable and service oriented paint people.
AT THE TOP OF RAPHUNE HILL, ST. THOMAS, VIRGIN ISLANDS. 775-1466

"I CAN'T COMPLAIN."

Don't you get tired of standing in a long line just to be abused at the other end?
You know, good service is pretty simple: give customers what they want. Do it efficiently. If they have a
question, have a staff that knows what they are talking about. Make sure you have enough inventory so they
don't waste a trip to your store. Give them a good price. Help them take their purchase to their car.
Tell them 'thank you'. And should for some unforseen reason, something go wrong,
have someone take care of the problem. *Right now!*

THE PAINT DEPOT

Coatings for every surface from the most knowledgeable and service oriented paint people.
AT THE TOP OF RAPHUNE HILL, ST. THOMAS, VIRGIN ISLANDS. 775-1466

WE MAKE HOUSE CALLS!

If you have trouble with a leaky roof and would like to get some help, call us. We'll be happy to go to your home,
climb up on your roof and tell you what might be the problem. We've been doing it for years.
As a matter of fact, no matter what paint or coating problem you may have, please call us. Most of the time
we can resolve your problem right on the phone. But if we can't, we'll go to your home and one of
our paint doctors will prescribe a solution for you.
And the cost? Why it's free, of course!

THE PAINT DEPOT

Coatings for every surface from the most knowledgeable and service oriented paint people.
AT THE TOP OF RAPHUNE HILL, ST. THOMAS, VIRGIN ISLANDS. 775-1466

MATCHMAKERS

If you're looking for the perfect match, then I'd like to introduce you to Ernest Ross, Bobby George, Kirsty Aitken, Mark Barczyk and Mike Perron. Boy, can they match paint colors! It doesn't matter where the paint chip comes from or what sample you bring in, these people will blend your paint for a match made in heaven or in this case, the Virgin Islands.
Voted by the fussiest, pickiest and most demanding people as *the* "best place" anywhere to the the right color match.

THE PAINT DEPOT

Coatings for every surface from the most knowledgeable and service oriented paint people.
AT THE TOP OF RAPHUNE HILL, ST. THOMAS, VIRGIN ISLANDS. 775-1466

IF TWO HEADS
ARE BETTER THAN ONE,
HOW ABOUT EIGHT?

Our eight staff members have more in-depth paint knowledge than anyone on island.
Which is why we have a heads up on solutions to your paint problems.

THE PAINT DEPOT

Coatings for every surface from the most knowledgeable and service oriented paint people.
AT THE TOP OF RAPHUNE HILL, ST. THOMAS, VIRGIN ISLANDS. 775-1466

HOW TO TRY ON A PAINT STORE.

If you're shopping for clothes, you'll try them on before buying. But what if you're looking to buy some paint? Then here are a few things to look for when shopping for a paint store:

Do they have a large inventory of paint?
We have the largest paint and roof coating inventory. Period.
Which means if you need something, it's here. On island.

Is there a knowledgeable staff?
Not only do we have people who really understand paint,
but we have more of them than anyone else. Seven, at last count.

Do they keep a record of your purchase on file?
We've been keeping records of every gallon of custom mixed paint for as long
as we've been in business. This comes in very handy
when you need to buy 'touch up paint' in the future.

So come on in and try us on for size.
We have 'off the rack' paint colors as well as 'custom made' paint colors.
Either way, this place will fit you like a glove.

THE PAINT DEPOT
Coatings for every surface from the most knowledgeable and service oriented paint people.
AT THE TOP OF RAPHUNE HILL, ST. THOMAS, VIRGIN ISLANDS. 775-1466

SELLING OUR CUSTOMER SERVICE.

Both these ads are selling the unique service we offer our customers.
Being located in one of the most visited place in the Caribbean, locals can readily identify with 'tourist traps'.

TOURIST TRAP!

Did you know that The Paint Depot is becoming a tourist trap?

When people come here, they want to see the principal points of interest.
In other words, anything we have here that they can't
get elsewhere---like the best customer service in
the Virgin Islands.

We'd like to put you in the capable hands of one of our specially
trained guided tour leaders (often referred to as "paint consultant").
He or she will lead you past awe-inspiring mountains of
Benjamin Moore paint, through unspoiled forests of Vulkem and GE Silicone
roof coatings, straight to our boundless oceans of paint
sundries. You will be asked to observe our efficent and
friendly manner.

No reservations required to arrange your tour.
And if you tell your tour guide Mike sent you,
there will be a free souvenir T-shirt after
your thrilling tour.

THE PAINT DEPOT

Coatings for every surface from the most knowledgeable and service oriented paint people.
AT THE TOP OF RAPHUNE HILL, ST. THOMAS, VIRGIN ISLANDS. 775-1466

PREPARATION H

It's that time of the year *again* when we prepare for hurricane season, the dreaded "H" word. So, if you have a leaky roof now, you know it's not going to get better. That's why you need to prepare it with the finest, most waterproof coating available, the Vulkem Urethane roofing system.

WHEN IT POURS, VULKEM REIGNS!
Why does Vulkem work when other roof coatings won't? Because Vulkem is formulated to withstand continuous immersion with no loss to its waterproofing ability. Vulkem also has the official NSF P151 certification. That makes Vulkem the safest for collecting drinking water from your roof.

UNMATCHED PERFORMANCE!
Vulkem has more adhesive strength, more tensile strength, more waterproofing ability than any water-based roof coating. Which is why Vulkem is on over two million square feet of roofs right here in the Virgin Islands.

WHEN ALL ELSE FAILS!
If you haven't found a solution to your leaky roof, then do what home owners architects and contractors do --- THEY VULKEM IT!

And if you do it now before the rainy season gets real bad, it won't be a pain in the you-know-what.

THE PAINT DEPOT
Coatings for every surface from the most knowledgeable and service oriented paint people.
AT THE TOP OF RAPHUNE HILL, ST. THOMAS, VIRGIN ISLANDS. 775-1466

AN INDUSTRIAL COATING SOLD IN ONLY ONE RETAIL OUTLET IN THE WORLD. OURS.

Vulkem is an industrial waterproofing deck coating which was only sold through distributors and large contractors in the US. We saw the need for such a product for flat roofs in the Virgin Islands. The manufacturer was a multi billion dollar chemical company.

It took a lot of phone calls, letters, personal visits and plain old bugging them before they gave us the rights to sell their product here in the U.S. Virgin Islands. They thought we were just too small a market for them. I believe they gave us the rights just to make us go away.

They asked for sales of at least $150,000. per year in order to maintain a distributorship.

Within two years we were selling about a million dollars a year on just one of their products.

The Paint Depot is the only retail outlet for this product anywhere on the planet. We were instrumental in developing and getting the NSF P151 water safety standard for the Vulkem system here in the Virgin Islands. (Since we collect drinking water on our roofs, water safety is critical.)

The manufacturing facility gave us an award of recognition for helping them develop this product for retail use.

Just as a comparison, the island of Puerto Rico, which is 60 miles west of the Virgin Islands has a Vulkem distributor. The population there is 4 million. The entire Virgin Islands has 100,000. You would think that the Puerto Rico Vulkem market would be 40 times more than us.

Wrong! We were outselling them by 400%!

THE MOST EXPENSIVE ROOF COATING IN THE VIRGIN ISLANDS...

...is the roof coating that doesn't work. You put it on your flat roof and it still leaks. So you coat again. And again. And again. When all else fails, get the Vulkem Urethane Roofing system. It works the first time. On flat roofs, in gutters, on continuous ponding water. And it comes with a guarantee. In writing. Vulkem also meets NSF P151 drinking water standards, the highest in the country.

THE PAINT DEPOT

Coatings for every surface from the most knowledgeable and service oriented paint people.
AT THE TOP OF RAPHUNE HILL, ST. THOMAS, VIRGIN ISLANDS. 775-1466

WHY ARE YOUR THOUGHTS ALWAYS IN THE GUTTER!

Probably because built-in roof gutters are the weakest part of your roofing system. Ponding water is the biggest enemy of water-based roof coatings. With the Vulkem Urethane system, there is no worry because ponding water will not affect it. And with our NSF P151 rating, Vukem is also the safest for collecting drinking water. So, get your mind out of the gutter and Vulkem it!

THE PAINT DEPOT

Coatings for every surface from the most knowledgeable and service oriented paint people.
AT THE TOP OF RAPHUNE HILL, ST. THOMAS, VIRGIN ISLANDS. 775-1466

WHEN THE BRAND BECOMES A VERB.

Sometimes, ads enter into our culture. You ask for a Kleenex, not a tissue paper. Pass me the Scotch Tape, not the sticky tape. You Google something.

We were able to create a verb with our newest roof coating. It worked so well and we promoted so heavily, that people asked their contractors to "Vulkem" their roofs, not coat it.

WHEN IT POURS, VULKEM REIGNS!

If you have a flat roof, Vulkem is the only system to consider. If you have a new roof under construction or a previously coated roof that you are tired of recoating every couple of years, then switch to the Vulkem roofing system. It has more adhesive strength, more tensile strength, more waterproofing ability, than any water-based roof coating. That's why no water-based roof coating can outperform it!

Vulkem is formulated to withstand continuous immersion in water with no loss to its waterproofing ability. The Vulkem roof coating system has been applied to more than two million square feet right here in the Virgin Islands. And Vulkem is safe for collecting drinking water from your roof.

So, if you haven't found a solution to your leaky roof, then do what property owners, architects and contractors do---THEY VULKEM IT!

THE PAINT DEPOT

Coatings for every surface from the most knowledgeable and service oriented paint people.
AT THE TOP OF RAPHUNE HILL, ST. THOMAS, VIRGIN ISLANDS. 775-1466

OUR OTHER TWO ROOF COATINGS.

In addition to Vulkem roof coating, we carry two other brands, a water based roof coating and a silicone roof coating. These are an important part of our business.

In the Virgin Islands, we collect rain water from our roof and save it in our cistern. Because people drink the water, roof coatings need to be safe. And because we live in a hurricane prone area, we get lots and lots of rain during hurricane season.

In 1996, the manufacturer of the previous brand of water-based roof coating we carried decided to take away our exclusive right to sell and make it available in other paint outlets in St. Thomas and St. John. We responded by finding another manu-

HAS YOUR LEAKING ROOF LEFT YOU UP A CREEK?

Well, here's your paddle.
The Vulkem Roofing system is formulated to withstand continuous immersion in water with no loss to its waterproofing ability. And its glossy surface will not promote mildew growth unlike porous water-based roof coatings. So, if you haven't found a solution to your leaky roof, then do what property owners, architects and contractors do---they Vulkem it!

THE PAINT DEPOT

Coatings for every surface from the most knowledgeable and service oriented paint people.
AT THE TOP OF RAPHUNE HILL, ST. THOMAS, VIRGIN ISLANDS. 775-1466

facturer who would private label for us. We called this brand "ToughKote".

We advertised and marketed heavily. A few months later, we dropped the other brand from our store. Within three years, the other brand was no longer sold in the US Virgin Islands. ToughKote then became the most popular water-based roof coating in St. Thomas and St. John.

We've had brands come and go but people shop at The Paint Depot first and trust us to recommend the right product.

On the following pages you'll see a sampling of how we targeted these products to our local market.

DRIP, DRIP, DRIP, DRIP, DRIP, DRIP, DRIP.....WOOOSHHHH!

You don't have to work at the CIA to know that all leaks get worse. Which is where we come in. We've got everything you need to take care of your leaky roof...the Vulkem Urethane system for flat roofs and ToughKote water-based roof coating for pitched roofs. Both are NSF approved for collecting drinking water for your cistern. Plus, we've got flashing compound, tape, brushes and rollers. If I were you, I'd come in right now while it's still only going drip, drip, drip.

THE PAINT DEPOT

Coatings for every surface from the most knowledgeable and service oriented paint people.
AT THE TOP OF RAPHUNE HILL, ST. THOMAS, VIRGIN ISLANDS. 775-1466

Selling the safety aspect
of our roof coatings.

THE DRINKS
ARE ON THE HOUSE.

All of our roof coatings are tested to NSF P151 standards
for collecting drinking water for your cistern.
Cheers!

THE PAINT DEPOT

Coatings for every surface from the most knowledgeable and service oriented paint people.
AT THE TOP OF RAPHUNE HILL, ST. THOMAS, VIRGIN ISLANDS. 775-1466

PROVE IT TO ME!

Quantify. I can't emphasize that enough. People assumed that the 'other' brand was better because it was around before we even opened our store. I took samples of their roof flashing and our roof flashing and embedded it in an ester tape on plywood.

To convince people, we asked them to tear it off the plywood.

The 'other' brand tore off easily while our brand took great effort, oftentimes the tape would tear first.

As I've said many times, quantify. Prove it.

"I DON'T CARE WHAT YOU TELL ME, I'M NOT CONVERTING TO YOUR BRAND OF ROOF COATING!"

You're a doubting Thomas or in our case down here, a doubting St. Thomian. We understand that switching brands is tough. You feel comfortable with what you're using. But consider this: if you need 4 buckets of roof coating to re-do your roof, you'll spend an extra $120.00 versus the other leading brand. Hey, that's a lot of extra money to leave up on the roof.

ToughKote roof coating has the very same NSF approval for the safe collection of water for your cistern. ToughKote also happens to be thicker. If you come into the store, just ask anyone here, "Go ahead, prove it to me!" and we'll let you test it yourself. We want to prove it in front of your very own eyes.

ToughKote roof coating has been a proven performer in the Virgin Islands for over 15 years. Contractors and homeowners love this product because it *really* works.

There's still time to be saved from spending too much money. Convert to ToughKote roof coating now.

THE PAINT DEPOT

Coatings for every surface from the most knowledgeable and service oriented paint people.
AT THE TOP OF RAPHUNE HILL, ST. THOMAS, VIRGIN ISLANDS. 775-1466

NO ONE EVER SAYS "I'M GOING TO TOUGHKOTE MY ROOF".

People use our competitors brand name instead.
But that's OK, we're the number two brand of water based roof coating which means we have to do it better.
For example, did you know that ToughKote roof coating has the very same NSF approval as the other guy? ToughKote roof coating also happens to be thicker. Come in the store and we'll demostrate it in front of your very own eyes.
ToughKote roof coating has been a proven performer in the Virgin Islands for the last 15 years. Contractors and homeowners love this product because it really works.

But here comes the best part---*the very best part*.
A five gallon pail of ToughKote roof coating costs about $30.00 *less* than the other brand.

Hey, that's a lot of extra money to leave up on your roof.
Shouldn't you start "ToughKoting" your roof?

THE PAINT DEPOT

Coatings for every surface from the most knowledgeable and service oriented paint people.
AT THE TOP OF RAPHUNE HILL, ST. THOMAS, VIRGIN ISLANDS. 775-1466

I remember people telling me ads have to be short. I've never believed that. It needs to be whatever it needs to be to make the sale.

No more, no less. If you are interested in something, you just can't get enough information. That's where long copy sells. You want to read everything about it.

WHICH BRAND OF FLASHING WILL YOU TRUST ON YOUR ROOF SEAMS?

ToughKote brand roof flashing has more adhesive strength,
much more, than the other leading brand.
And when you're taping seams on your roof, you want
the stuff to really stick to your plywood.
I've gots lots and lots of "us versus them" samples
in the store for you to do a side by side comparison
for yourself.
It'll make a believer out of you.

Oh, by the way, did I mention that our flashing costs about
$30.00 less per bucket?
As if that should matter.

THE PAINT DEPOT

Coatings for every surface from the most knowledgeable and service oriented paint people.
AT THE TOP OF RAPHUNE HILL, ST. THOMAS, VIRGIN ISLANDS. 775-1466

THREE REVELATIONS AND A BRIBE.

You can learn a lot about roof coating by coming in to The Paint Depot. The first thing you'll learn is that Vulkem is the only roof coating for flat roofs that is NSF approved for collecting drinking water for your cistern. Second thing you'll learn is that our ToughKote water based roof coating is about $30.00 less a pail than the other leading brand. The third thing you'll learn is that our ToughKote roof flashing has much more adhesive strength than the other guys brand. And to prove just how much more adhesive strength our flashing has, we'd like to bribe you with a free T-shirt. Just come on in and say "Let me compare your ToughKote flashing to the other guys." Oh, and if the bribe bothers you, just tell us "I don't need your T-shirt. I'm here on business. Period. Just prove to me your flashing is better." We'll understand.

THE PAINT DEPOT

Coatings for every surface from the most knowledgeable and service oriented paint people.

AT THE TOP OF RAPHUNE HILL, ST. THOMAS, VIRGIN ISLANDS. 775-1466

DEATH AND TAXES.

There's also one more inevitable thing that happens to us down here, hurricane season.
And that means rain...lots and lots of it. Which means now, *right now,* is the time to prepare your roof for it.
We have everything you need to fix, repair, recoat and patch your roof. ToughKote water-based roof
coating for your pitched roof and Vulkem urethane roof coating for flat roofs. By the way,
our ToughKote roof coating costs $48. LESS PER BUCKET than the other leading brand.

THE PAINT DEPOT

Coatings for every surface from the most knowledgeable and service oriented paint people.
AT THE TOP OF RAPHUNE HILL, ST. THOMAS, VIRGIN ISLANDS. 775-1466

STRETCHING THE TRUTH

A lot of silicone roof coatings will tell you they are the "best". Well, I say they're stretching the truth.

The hard fact is this:

When it comes to elongation (the ability of a roof coating to stretch and bridge cracks, GE ENDURIS 3500 Silicone roof coating has an elongation rating of 542%! Compare that to other silicone roof coatings with only 250% to 306%.

Besides being able to bridge cracks better, GE ENDURIS Silicone roof coating has better tear resistance, superior UV resistance, is unaffected by standing water, has Energy Star rating and, of course, is NSF rated to collect drinking water for your cistern.

So, when it's time to coat your roof, come to The Paint Depot, official distributor of GE ENDURIS Silicone roof coatings.

Hey, why settle for just regular elongation when you can get superior eloooooooooongation.

THE PAINT DEPOT
Distributors of GE ENDURIS 100% SILICONE roof coatings.
AL COHEN PLAZA, (TOP OF RAPHUNE HILL) ST. THOMAS, VIRGIN ISLANDS.
775-1466

IT'S IN THE DETAILS.

Like soap, you need to find some unique selling point for your products. This silicone roof coating had more elongation than other competitors. And that makes a huge difference when bridging cracks on roofs.

Find the uniqueness and exploit it.

YOU SAY TOMATO.

AND I SAY TOMAHTOE.

YOU SAY YOU WANT A GREAT ROOF COATING.
And I say Toughkote water-based roof coating.

YOU SAY YOU WANT A GREAT PRICE.
And I say our ToughKote roof coating will save you
over $60.00 per bucket over the other leading brand!

YOU SAY YOU WANT THE BEST FLASHING.
And I say Toughkote flashing has better, no, make that
much better adhesion than the other leading brand.
And ours is over $70.00 per bucket less than theirs!

Paint Deepoe or Paint Dehpoh, no matter how you pronouce it,
this is the place to get great products, incredible service and low prices.

THE PAINT DEPOT

Coatings for every surface from the most knowledgeable and service oriented paint people.
AT THE TOP OF RAPHUNE HILL, ST. THOMAS, VIRGIN ISLANDS. 775-1466

A BETTER MOUSETRAP.

There is an old adage, "Build a better mousetrap and the world will beat a path to your door." That's naive thinking. I think you need to build a *better path* to your door *and the*n the world will find out about your better mousetrap.

Building that better path to me was advertising. And there's nothing like a legitimate, honest product endorsement. Corporations pay millions for it.

I approached people who used our Vulkem Urethane roofing system and asked could I run an ad with their endorsement. When you have a product that actually did as promised and solved very expensive leak problems on roofs, it was an easy sell.

It wasn't just one endorsement, it was twelve of them, thirteen if you count mine.

    And when our customers came to look at our better mousetrap, it really was better.

"We've had continuous leaking problems at the Winston Rhymer Community Center. Since the Vulkem was applied, there hasn't been a single leak."

Alphonse Nibbs Sr., Assistant Commission, Housing, Parks & Recreation.

THE PAINT DEPOT

Coatings for every surface from the most knowledgeable and service oriented paint people.
AT THE TOP OF RAPHUNE HILL, ST. THOMAS, VIRGIN ISLANDS. 775-1466

"The Vulkem system is bullet-proof! It's the only thing I'll recommend to use on any roof."

*Larry Witkop,
S.O.S. Maintenance.*

THE PAINT DEPOT

Coatings for every surface from the most knowledgeable and service oriented paint people.
AT THE TOP OF RAPHUNE HILL, ST. THOMAS, VIRGIN ISLANDS. 775-1466

"We specify the
Vulkem urethane roofing
system on all flat roofs for
one simple reason. It works."

*Leroy Smith, John Woods,
Jaredian Design.*

THE PAINT DEPOT

Coatings for every surface from the most knowledgeable and service oriented paint people.
AT THE TOP OF RAPHUNE HILL, ST. THOMAS, VIRGIN ISLANDS. 775-1466

"We had the Vulkem system applied on 10,000 sq. ft. of roofs in June 1996 and it's as shiny and clean as the day it was installed. And no leaks! This is an impressive product."

*Frank Barry,
Sapphire West Condo Association.*

THE PAINT DEPOT

Coatings for every surface from the most knowledgeable and service oriented paint people.
AT THE TOP OF RAPHUNE HILL, ST. THOMAS, VIRGIN ISLANDS. 775-1466

"The downtown Scotia Bank building had persistent leaking problems. You name the coating and it's up on that roof. The only thing that solved the problem was the Vulkem roof system."

*Tracy Roberts,
Architect.*

VULKEM
HIGH PERFORMANCE
URETHANE ROOFING SYSTEM

THE PAINT DEPOT
Coatings for every surface from the most knowledgeable and service oriented paint people.
AT THE TOP OF RAPHUNE HILL, ST. THOMAS, VIRGIN ISLANDS. 775-1466

"We first used the Vulkem system to line the gutters and coat the flat roof at the Lucinda Millin Home. We now use it every chance we can because this stuff really works."

*Steve Lammens,
Custom Builders Inc.*

THE PAINT DEPOT

Coatings for every surface from the most knowledgeable and service oriented paint people.
AT THE TOP OF RAPHUNE HILL, ST. THOMAS, VIRGIN ISLANDS. 775-1466

"I'm specifying the Vulkem roof system both flat and pitched roofs. It's a really great product."

*Michael Helm,
Architect, Tortola, B.V.I.*

VULKEM
HIGH PERFORMANCE URETHANE ROOFING SYSTEM

THE PAINT DEPOT
Coatings for every surface from the most knowledgeable and service oriented paint people.
AT THE TOP OF RAPHUNE HILL, ST. THOMAS, VIRGIN ISLANDS. 775-1466

"I've applied over 100,000 sq. ft. of Vulkem. I won't use any other roof coating because this stuff really works."

*Paul Crosby,
P&C Roofing.*

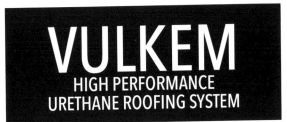

THE PAINT DEPOT

Coatings for every surface from the most knowledgeable and service oriented paint people.
AT THE TOP OF RAPHUNE HILL, ST. THOMAS, VIRGIN ISLANDS. 775-1466

"We used the Vulkem system on a number of flat roofs at Oswald Harris Court Housing and found this stuff to be incredible! I intend to use and specify it every chance I can."

*Curtis Elcock,
Neon Construction Inc.*

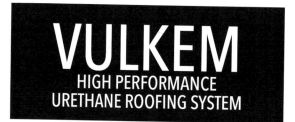

VULKEM
HIGH PERFORMANCE URETHANE ROOFING SYSTEM

THE PAINT DEPOT

Coatings for every surface from the most knowledgeable and service oriented paint people.
AT THE TOP OF RAPHUNE HILL, ST. THOMAS, VIRGIN ISLANDS. 775-1466

"The Vulkem liquid roofing system is the finest I've ever used. I can never go back to water-based roof coatings again."

*Gerry Roy,
Roy's Construction Inc.*

VULKEM
HIGH PERFORMANCE
URETHANE ROOFING SYSTEM

THE PAINT DEPOT

Coatings for every surface from the most knowledgeable and service oriented paint people.
AT THE TOP OF RAPHUNE HILL, ST. THOMAS, VIRGIN ISLANDS. 775-1466

"We used the Vulkem system on the flat roof at Frank's Bake Shop. I'm impressed with this tough product and would recommend it to anyone."

*Lubin Roberts,
Lubin Roberts Construction Ltd.*

THE PAINT DEPOT
Coatings for every surface from the most knowledgeable and service oriented paint people.
AT THE TOP OF RAPHUNE HILL, ST. THOMAS, VIRGIN ISLANDS. 775-1466

THINK SMALL.

To my mind, the greatest ads ever written were for Volkswagen in the 1960's. "Think Small". What a headline! Not only was the ad agency brilliant, it would never have flown without a smart client to approve it.

When Benjamin Moore came out with small paint samples for testing colors at home, my mind immediately thought of the "Think Small" ad campaign.

I took the concept, including some other famous Volkswagen headlines and designed them to look like those vintage '60's VW ads.

And it worked beautifully with our small paint samples.

Think small.

Doesn't it just bug you to buy an entire gallon or even a quart can of paint just to use two ounces of it for a color sample on your wall?

And then your mate tells you the color is ugly!

Well, Benjamin-Moore has come out with a really small idea to solve this problem: two ounce jars of pre-tinted, ready to use paint color samples.

We've got those little jars in 260 of Benjamin Moore's most popular colors.

They're in stock and ready to go.

One jar is enough to do about four square feet. Perfect for that great big color idea of yours.

THE PAINT DEPOT
775-1466
ST. THOMAS, VI

It's ugly.

You're looking for that perfect shade of yellow but you had to buy an entire gallon of paint just to put a 2 ounce sample on your wall.

And then you find out your perfect shade of yellow turns out to be pretty ugly!

Well, Benjamin-Moore has come out with a really attractive way to save you some money: two ounce jars of pre-tinted, ready to use paint color samples.

We've got those little jars in 260 of Benjamin Moore's most popular colors.

They're in stock, ready to go. One jar is enough to do about four square feet. Perfect for that beautiful color idea of yours.

THE PAINT DEPOT
775-1466
ST. THOMAS, VI

Lemon.

You're looking for that perfect shade of yellow but you had to buy a 32 ounce can of paint just to put a 2 ounce sample on your wall.

And then you find out your perfect shade of yellow turns out to be a lemon.

Well, Benjamin-Moore has come out with a really fresh idea to save you some money: two ounce jars of pre-tinted, ready to use paint color samples.

We've got those little jars in 260 of Benjamin Moore's most popular colors. They're in stock and ready to go.

One jar is enough to do about four square feet. Perfect for those fruitful color ideas of yours.

THE PAINT DEPOT
775-1466
ST. THOMAS, VI

TYING IN TO THE MEDIA.

We advertised weekly in FOCUS, the local TV listing insert in our daily newspaper. I've always believed in tying the ad message to the medium. You'll get better readership.

These ad headlines take advantage of top TV shows, movies and special TV events that were popular at the time. Since you are browsing the TV listing section of the paper, ad headlines that mimic your favorite TV show creates better readership of the ad.

AMERICAN IDLE!

If you don't know what to do this weekend, then change the color of your bedroom. We have over 5000 colors that will sing out to you like 'blue suede shoes', 'yellow brick road', 'good vibrations', 'misty' and 'silent night' (yes, these are real color names.) And the cost? Two gallons of Martin-Senour Proline Premium interior latex semi-gloss, white or pastel, will cost you $34.12. Add a decent 2" paint brush, one 1/2" roller sleeve, one heavy duty roller paint frame and a sturdy plastic paint tray and you're at $45.93. It's a small price to pay to be a film star...paint film that is.

THE PAINT DEPOT

Coatings for every surface from the most knowledgeable and service oriented paint people. AT THE TOP OF RAPHUNE HILL, ST. THOMAS, VIRGIN ISLANDS. 775-1466

007

Whenever as new James Bond movie or a TV station would run all the James Bond movies in a week, we'd use this ad.

"SHAKEN, NOT STIRRED."

(James Bond's response when asked how he wanted his Benjamin-Moore custom paint mixed.)

THE PAINT DEPOT

Coatings for every surface from the most knowledgeable and service oriented paint people.
AT THE TOP OF RAPHUNE HILL, ST. THOMAS, VIRGIN ISLANDS. 775-1466

I'M SINGING IN THE RAIN!

Must be someone with a Vulkem Urethane roofing system.

THE PAINT DEPOT

Coatings for every surface from the most knowledgeable and service oriented paint people.

AT THE TOP OF RAPHUNE HILL, ST. THOMAS, VIRGIN ISLANDS. 775-1466

This ran when The Sopranos were a big hit.

BADA BING!

You getting wacked with high roof coating prices? Then foooget about going anywhere else but here.
Our ToughKote water-based roof coating is NSF tested for safety and has been applied to hundreds of thousands
of square feet of roofs over the last 10 years. But here's the best part. The very best part.
Our roof coating costs $48.00 LESS PER BUCKET than the other popular brand of roof coating.
With savings like that, we won't need to make you an offer you can't refuse.

THE PAINT DEPOT

Coatings for every surface from the most knowledgeable and service oriented paint people.
AT THE TOP OF RAPHUNE HILL, ST. THOMAS, VIRGIN ISLANDS. 775-1466

C.S.I.

(COATING SCENE INVESTIGATION)

If you paint over a very chalky surface, it's a crime. Why? Because your paint job won't last long before it starts peeling. Which is where we come in. We want to make sure that you get the longest life possible for your paint by helping you select the best coating system. From prep to primer to finish coat. And the evidence of a good paint job is when we don't see you back here for quite some time. Unless of course, you want to change the color again.

THE PAINT DEPOT

Coatings for every surface from the most knowledgeable and service oriented paint people.
AT THE TOP OF RAPHUNE HILL, ST. THOMAS, VIRGIN ISLANDS. 775-1466

THE WIZARD OF AHHS!

If you're looking for a superb custom matched color, then visit one of our wizards.
Because no matter what sample you bring in, we'll blend your paint to bring out all the "oohs" and "ahhs".
Voted by the fussiest, pickiest and most demanding
homeowners and contractors alike as *the best place anywhere*
to get the right color matches.

THE PAINT DEPOT

Coatings for every surface from the most knowledgeable and service oriented paint people.
AT THE TOP OF RAPHUNE HILL, ST. THOMAS, VIRGIN ISLANDS. 775-1466

I still run this ad to this day. As of this writing, Mission: Impossible #7, part 1 is just coming out which means it's time to run it again.

MISSION: POSSIBLE!

YOUR ASSIGNMENT: find a paint that's not only mildew-resistant but *mildew proof!* Zinsser's PermaWhite exterior or interior paint is the only house paint guaranteed to prevent mildew growth for 5 years when two coats are applied according to label directions. It's also extremely durable. So, for your next painting mission, get the coating that's *mildew-proof,* Zinsser's Perma-White exterior or interior paint.

THE PAINT DEPOT

Coatings for every surface from the most knowledgeable and service oriented paint people.
AT THE TOP OF RAPHUNE HILL, ST. THOMAS, VIRGIN ISLANDS. 775-1466

WHAT WOMEN WANT!

Is what The Paint Depot has.
The right colors. Great prices. Exceptional service from a very knowledgeable staff.
One of the largest coatings selection and inventory in the Caribbean.
Attention to detail. Really nice people.
And we listen. *Attentively.*

THE PAINT DEPOT

Coatings for every surface from the most knowledgeable and service oriented paint people.
AT THE TOP OF RAPHUNE HILL, ST. THOMAS, VIRGIN ISLANDS. 775-1466

THE COLOR PURPLE.

As well as thousands of other Martin Senour paint colors are available at The Paint Depot.

THE PAINT DEPOT

Coatings for every surface from the most knowledgeable and service oriented paint people.

AT THE TOP OF RAPHUNE HILL, ST. THOMAS, VIRGIN ISLANDS. 775-1466

JEOPARDY FOR PAINTERS!

CATEGORY: ROOF COATINGS

THE ANSWER:
"It's the absolute best roof coating you can use on a flat roof."

THE QUESTION:
"What is the Vulkem Urethane Roofing System?"

CATEGORY: SAVING MONEY

THE ANSWER:
"This water-based roof coating sells for over $60.00 LESS per
5 gallon pail than the other leading brand."

THE QUESTION:
"What is ToughKote Elastomeric roof coating?"

CATEGORY: GREAT SERVICE

THE ANSWER:
"The most knowledgeable and service oriented paint and roof coating people in the Virgin Islands."

THE QUESTION:
"Who are Mark, 'Bobby', 'Copter', Ernest, Mike, Kirsty and Linda?"

FINAL JEOPARDY ANSWER:

"Seven thousand eight hundred and fifty six."

THE QUESTION:
"How many Paint Depot customers have a written record of their custom mixed paint colors on file there?"

THE PAINT DEPOT

Coatings for every surface from the most knowledgeable and service oriented paint people.
AT THE TOP OF RAPHUNE HILL, ST. THOMAS, VIRGIN ISLANDS. 775-1466

THE WIZARD OF ODDS!

We've got a bunch of odd mixed paints that we'd like to make disappear. And with the Easter long weekend coming up, it's a perfect time for doing that painting project. By the way, did I mention the price?
Free. Just come in, buy anything, even a .50 cent brush, and then
choose from our selection of odd mistinted paints.
Limit one free gallon per customer. Offer ends April 19, 2003.

THE PAINT DEPOT

Coatings for every surface from the most knowledgeable and service oriented paint people.
AT THE TOP OF RAPHUNE HILL, ST. THOMAS, VIRGIN ISLANDS. 775-1466

THE RIGHT STUFF!

We've got what it takes to make things right. Like more experienced paint people (eight of us), more inventory than you can shake a paint stick at, more color selection (over 5,000) and more paint stuff than any other place on island. And when it comes to color matching, we are light years ahead. Hey, you don't have to be a rocket scientist to know this is the place to get great products, incredible service and down to earth prices.

THE PAINT DEPOT

Coatings for every surface from the most knowledgeable and service oriented paint people.

AT THE TOP OF RAPHUNE HILL, ST. THOMAS, VIRGIN ISLANDS. 775-1466

This was a natural headline for 2001.

2001: A ROOF ODYSSEY

If your year starts with a leak, end it with the Vulkem Urethane roofing system.
Simply the finest and most waterproof liquid applied roof coating.
And it comes with a written warranty...one that'll hold water.

THE PAINT DEPOT

Coatings for every surface from the most knowledgeable and service oriented paint people.
AT THE TOP OF RAPHUNE HILL, ST. THOMAS, VIRGIN ISLANDS. 775-1466

PAINT YOUR WAGON.

Your sedan, coupe, SUV or taxi van. That's right, we custom mix high quality car paints for any of the body repair shops in St. Thomas. So, if you're planning to paint your wagon, insist on Martin Senour automotive finishes from the people who *really* know paints.

THE PAINT DEPOT

Coatings for every surface from the most knowledgeable and service oriented paint people.
AT THE TOP OF RAPHUNE HILL, ST. THOMAS, VIRGIN ISLANDS. 775-1466

CARTOON ADS.

If you read every one of our ads that we run in a year, you would not see the same ad more than twice. This has created a loyal following of readers, just like a weekly comic strip. I can't tell you how often I was stopped by people in the street or in the store and have them repeat the headline of the current ad we were running. One customer told me she was collecting all my ads.

So, when I thought of the comic strip analogy, I also thought, why not actually do one.

This series ran for four months and then I stopped. I can't tell you why, but my gut said I needed to go back to my simple design.

XXXXXXXLARGE

Shopping at the largest paint store, which we just happen to be, means absolutely nothing. Unless, of course, you are passionate about customer service, which we also just happen to be. This store is a locally owned and operated place that happens to have more experienced paint people, more color choices, more inventory
and paint accessories than you can shake a paint stick at. Plus incredible service.
So, if you're looking for the right paint store size for all your needs, XXXXXXXXL is the perfect fit.

THE PAINT DEPOT, ST. THOMAS, VI 775-1466

A GOOD STORM SEASON STARTS WITH A SMART PRE-SEASON!

Well, this is the time of the year when heavy, long lasting rains will be coming down. So, if you don't take care of that leak NOW, it's only going to get worse. We've got everything you need to fix a leak, repair a crack or coat the whole roof. Our ToughKote water-based roof coating and flashing compound has been successfully applied in the Caribbean for over 25 years. And if it's the ultimate protection you're looking for, ask us about GE 100% silicone roof coating or the Vulkem Roofing System. You'll always score BIG with Team Paint Depot.

THE PAINT DEPOT, ST. THOMAS, VI 775-1466

WE ARE NOT 'THE LUMBER DEPOT'

We don't sell lumber, nails or fridges. We don't have electric tools, outdoor furniture or plumbing supplies. We sell coatings, that's it. For every surface. And we're experts at it. So, if you're looking for <u>real</u> advice, quality products and exceptional service for your next paint or roof coating project, talk to the people who deal in only one thing...coatings. *No one knows their stuff like we do.*

THE PAINT DEPOT, ST. THOMAS, VI   775-1466

HOW IS IT THAT 50% OF OUR STAFF IS LEFT HANDED?

With less than 15% of the regular population left handed, how is it that our staff is neatly divided between left and right handed people? Well, there was a good reason why we hired our people that way. You see, on one hand we are very liberal with our low prices and on the other hand we are very conservative when it comes to selecting great products. But when it comes to giving great service, we become bipartisan and give you the benefit of both our left and right handed thinking.

THE PAINT DEPOT, ST. THOMAS, VI 775-1466

IN THE TROPICS YOU NEED A GOOD COAT.

Got a flat roof? For that you need the ultimate coat for your roof, the GE Enduris 100% Silicone roofing system. Looking for a coat for your pitched roof? Try our ToughKote water-based roof coating. Need a protective coat for your exterior walls? Use our elastomeric coat system. It can withstand wind driven rains up to 98 mph! And if it's a beatiful coat for your inside walls that you are seeking, then Benjamin Moore has thousands of the latest style colors to choose from. Come in and browse. We have every coat size: pint, quart, gallon, 5 gallon.

THE PAINT DEPOT, ST. THOMAS, VI   775-1466

AN ITSY BITSY LEAK.

They all start out the same way. An itsy, bitsy leak in your roof. And it only really leaks when it's raining more than 5 minutes. Well, this is the time of the year when heavy, long lasting rains will be coming down. So, if you don't take care of that leak NOW, it's only going to get worse. We've got everything you need to fix a leak, repair a crack or coat the whole roof. Our ToughKote water-based roof coating and flashing compound has been successfully applied in the Caribbean for over 25 years. And if it's the ultimate protection you're looking for, ask us about GE 100% silicone roof coating or the Vulkem Roofing System.

THE PAINT DEPOT, ST. THOMAS, VI   775-1466

VOTE FOR
BEN 'JAMMIN' MOORE!

It's election time again! It's very important to vote tomorrow!
When you cast your vote for "Paint Commissioner", be sure to re-elect
Ben 'Jammin' Moore, better known as Benjamin Moore.
As the most colorful candidate in the Virgin Islands, he'll represent your home with
outstanding quality and value for many years to come.
Stop by his campaign headquarters located at the top of Raphune Hill in St. Thomas.

THE PAINT DEPOT, ST. THOMAS, VI 775-1466

SMALLER ADS.

Advertising rates are always going up. The newspaper had a deal where you could repeat the same ad twice in a week and get the second ad at half price. So, we experimented in reducing the size of the ad from 4" high to 3" high. We moved the logo to the right instead of the bottom. By doing this, I could still get the same copy and impact and run two ads a week without it costing me that much more.

This is the style of ads we've been using for the last ten years. It also runs in the digital edition of the newspaper with the logo in red.

DON'T PUNISH YOURSELF WITH ONLY 50 SHADES OF GRAY.

THE PAINT DEPOT
ST. THOMAS, V.I.
775-1466

We have hundreds of shades of gray and blue and yellow and green. And if it's a special color you need matched, bring the sample to us and we'll color match it perfectly. Our new color selector room has more colors and of course the absolute best paint advice on island.
Isn't it painfully obvious that The Paint Depot is THE place for paint?

Coatings for every surface from the most knowledgeable and service oriented paint people.

THE SHOELACE DEPOT.
THE GOLDFISH DEPOT.
THE NAIL POLISH DEPOT.

I don't know about you, but I like to shop at places where people really know their stuff. Here at The Paint Depot, we sell coatings, that's it. For every surface. And we're experts at it. So, if you need <u>real</u> advice, quality products and exceptional service, talk to the people who deal in only one thing...coatings. *No one knows their stuff like we do.*

THE PAINT DEPOT
ST. THOMAS, V.I.
775-1466

Coatings for every surface from the most knowledgeable and service oriented paint people.

I'M DREAMING OF A...

...white Christmas,
red Christmas,
blue Christmas,
yellow Christmas,
or any other color you can think of Christmas!
Have it any way you want with Benjamin Moore quality paints.

THE PAINT DEPOT
ST. THOMAS, V.I.
775-1466

Coatings for every surface from the most knowledgeable and service oriented paint people.

ELOOOOOONGATION.

When it comes to elongation (the ability of a roof coating to stretch and bridge cracks, GE ENDURIS 3500 Silicone roof coating has an elongation rating of 542%! Compare that to other silicone roof coatings with only 250% to 306%. In addition to being able to bridge cracks better, GE ENDURIS Silicone roof coating has better tear resistance, superior UV resistance, is unaffected by standing water, has Energy Star rating and, of course, is certified to NSF P151 standards.

Why settle for regular elongation when you can get elooooooooooongation with GE Silicone Roof Coating.

Coatings for every surface from the most knowledgeable and service oriented paint people.

DON'T STOP THE CARNIVAL!

It's still on at The Paint Depot! Our colorful troop of paint mixers will dazzle you as they tramp down the aisles, whip that gallon in the tint machine and then spin it round and round to get your perfect color.

You are, of course, welcome to dance by the cash register as your paint is getting ready.

Coatings for every surface from the most knowledgeable and service oriented paint people.

YOU MUST BE AT LEAST 18 YEARS OLD TO READ THIS AD!

Let's face it, if you're under 18, you're really not into painting. I know I wasn't. But now that I'm older, painting lets me create wonderful moods in my home. Whether it's a restful shade of green or a bold, vibrant yellow, I can always count on The Paint Depot to give me quality products, great service and low prices.

Coatings for every surface from the most knowledgeable and service oriented paint people.

THE PAINT DEPOT
ST. THOMAS, V.I.
775-1466

WANT TO IMPRESS YOUR MOM ON MOTHER'S DAY?

If you're looking to impress, and I mean, *really* impress, then surprise your mom by painting a room in her favorite color.
Flowers will wilt in a few days but our Benjamin Moore colors will last a very, very long time.

Coatings for every surface from the most knowledgeable and service oriented paint people.

THE PAINT DEPOT
ST. THOMAS, V.I.
775-1466

A PLACE THAT SELLS PAINT OR A PAINT STORE?

I don't know about you, but I like to shop at places where people really know their stuff. Here at The Paint Depot, we sell coatings, that's it. For every surface. And we're experts at it. So, if you need <u>real</u> advice, quality products and exceptional service, talk to the people who deal in only one thing...coatings. *No one knows their stuff like we do.*

Coatings for every surface from the most knowledgeable and service oriented paint people.

RE-ELECT BEN "JAMMIN" MOORE AND GET A BALANCED BUDGET!

When you cast your vote, be sure to re-elect Ben "Jammin" Moore as the Virgin Islands Paint Commissioner. He's got great pricing, an honest product and has served the community for 27 years. Your vote means your personal budget won't go into a deficit.

Coatings for every surface from the most knowledgeable and service oriented paint people.

A GOOD STORM SEASON STARTS WITH A SMART PRE-SEASON.

Well, it won't be long before heavy, long lasting rains will be coming down. So, if you don't take care of that leak NOW, it's only going to get worse. We've got everything you need to fix a leak, repair a crack or coat the whole roof. Our ToughKote water-based roof coating and flashing compound has been successfully applied in the Caribbean for over 26 years. And if it's the ultimate protection you're looking for, ask us about GE 100% silicone roof coating or the Vulkem Roofing System. You'll always score BIG with Team Paint Depot.

Coatings for every surface from the most knowledgeable and service oriented paint people.

SLIM CHANCE.

When you buy paint that is mildew-*resistant*, your chances are slim of stopping mildew. Especially if you live high up in the hills. What you need is a mildew-*proof* paint. Zinsser's PermaGuard mildew-proof paint is your best chance of controlling mildew.

So, if you're looking for a mildew-proof paint that's better than Zinsser PermaGuard, here's what I have to say about that: fat chance.

Coatings for every surface from the most knowledgeable and service oriented paint people.

★★★★★

If you're looking for a five star film, (paint film that is), then you've come to the right place. Our full line of Benjamin Moore paints provide the toughest, most beautiful paint film around. So direct yourself to The Paint Depot for great products, incredible service and low prices.

Coatings for every surface from the most knowledgeable and service oriented paint people.

THE PAINT DEPOT
ST. THOMAS, V.I.
775-1466

COME WATCH THE
BEN 'JAMMIN' MOORE PAINT SHOW!

Critics are calling it the most colorful show in St. Thomas! And it's on from 7:30 am to 4:30 pm Monday to Friday and 7:30 am to 2 pm on Saturdays. Come in and watch the show LIVE!

Coatings for every surface from the most knowledgeable and service oriented paint people.

THE PAINT DEPOT
ST. THOMAS, V.I.
775-1466

WE ARE NOT 'THE LUMBER DEPOT'

We don't sell lumber, nails or fridges. We don't have electric tools, outdoor furniture or plumbing supplies. We sell coatings, that's it. For every surface. And we're experts at it. So, if you're looking for real advice, quality products and exceptional service for your next paint or roof coating project, talk to the people who deal in only one thing... coatings. *No one knows their stuff like we do.*

Coatings for every surface from the most knowledgeable and service oriented paint people.

THE PAINT DEPOT
ST. THOMAS, V.I.
775-1466

WE ARE NOT 'THE PLUMBING DEPOT'

We don't sell lumber, nails or fridges. We don't have electric tools, outdoor furniture or plumbing supplies. We sell coatings, that's it. For every surface. And we're experts at it. So, if you're looking for real advice, quality products and exceptional service for your next paint or roof coating project, talk to the people who deal in only one thing...coatings.
No one knows their stuff like we do.

Coatings for every surface from the most knowledgeable and service oriented paint people.

THE PAINT DEPOT
ST. THOMAS, V.I.
775-1466

WE ARE NOT 'THE ELECTRICAL DEPOT'

We don't sell lumber, nails or fridges. We don't have electric tools, outdoor furniture or plumbing supplies. We sell coatings, that's it. For every surface. And we're experts at it. So, if you're looking for <u>real</u> advice, quality products and exceptional service for your roof coating project, talk to the people who deal in only one thing...coatings.
No one knows their stuff like we do.

Coatings for every surface from the most knowledgeable and service oriented paint people.

THE PAINT DEPOT
ST. THOMAS, V.I.
775-1466

"YOUR WIFE IS *REALLY* HOT!"

And I'll tell you why.
It's your roof coating. Very dark colored roof coatings attract the sun's heat. And that can make your home 15 degrees hotter inside. Light colors, especially white, reflects the sun's rays and will keep you cooler. All our roof coatings have very high reflective values for the white versions which makes them super cool. I know, you'd like to have a little color on your roof, but if you don't want you and your wife to be hot, tone down on the roof coating color and keep your cool.

Coatings for every surface from the most knowledgeable and service oriented paint people.

THE PAINT DEPOT
ST. THOMAS, V.I.
775-1466

ST. PATRICK'S DAY.

Every year for the last 20 years, I run a version of this ad the week before St. Patrick's Day.

I pick the names of a couple of people I like and use them in the ad, first names only. And of course, I mail them a copy of the newspaper where it appeared.

In this example, Jack is my brother and Sharon is my sister-in-law.

FITZHENRY, FITZPATRICK, FITZJACK, FITZSHARON, FITZEVERYBODY!

If you're wondering what to do on St. Patrick's Day, you might consider painting something green at your house. Benjamin Moore has hundreds of beautiful shades of green to choose from. Come in and see us. We've got a paint that fits virtually any budget.

Coatings for every surface from the most knowledgeable and service oriented paint people.

THE PAINT DEPOT
ST. THOMAS, V.I.
775-1466

FITZHENRY, FITZPATRICK, FITZKATHY, FITZTRACY, FITZEVERYBODY!

If you're wondering what to do on St. Patrick's Day, you might consider painting something green at your house. Benjamin Moore has hundreds of beautiful shades of green to choose from. Come in and see us. We've got a paint that fits virtually any budget.

Coatings for every surface from the most knowledgeable and service oriented paint people.

THE PAINT DEPOT
ST. THOMAS, V.I.
775-1466

FITZHENRY, FITZPATRICK, FITZMIKE, FITZLINDA, FITZEVERYBODY!

If you're wondering what to do on St. Patrick's Day, you might consider painting something green at your house. Benjamin Moore has hundreds of beautiful shades of green to choose from. Come in and see us. We've got a paint that fits virtually any budget.

Coatings for every surface from the most knowledgeable and service oriented paint people.

THE PAINT DEPOT
ST. THOMAS, V.I.
775-1466

COLOR SELECTION.

Most paint stores will offer you single paint chips. We would let the customer take the entire fan deck home with them.

WHEN CHOOSING A PAINT COLOR, ARE YOU PLAYING WITH A FULL DECK?

Have you ever picked a few color paint chips, taken them home to make sure it matches the couch only to realize it's not quite the right shade? Paint chip samples are nice but wouldn't it be much, much better if you had every single color available to you, right in your home? You bet it would! So instead of relying on the luck of the draw, we're offering you a sane way to approach color selection...we'll let you bring _all_ of our paint colors right to your home! Just tell us "I have no idea what color I want!" and we'll loan you the complete Martin-Senour color fan deck collection. With well over one thousand five hundred colors to choose from, matching your couch or rug or tiles or anything else will be so much easier. What a deal!

THE PAINT DEPOT

COATINGS FOR EVERY SURFACE FROM THE MOST KNOWLEDGEABLE AND SERVICE ORIENTED PAINT PEOPLE.
AL COHEN PLAZA, ST. THOMAS, VIRGIN ISLANDS. 775-1466

ELECTION DAY.

Here's an ad that I run the week before any election, whether local or federal.

You need to ask yourself if your ad has a timeless qualify. Could it of run 20 years ago or 20 years into the future? In my books, that's what makes a great ad idea.

REPUBLICANS AND DEMOCRATS HAVE ALWAYS AGREED ON ONE THING...

...that The Paint Depot is **THE** place to buy paint and roof coatings.

Come in anytime and experience politically correct service, liberal prices and conservative product values.

THE PAINT DEPOT

Coatings for every surface from the most knowledgeable and service oriented paint people.
AT THE TOP OF RAPHUNE HILL, ST. THOMAS, VIRGIN ISLANDS. 775-1466

CLASSIFIED PERSONAL ADS.

There was a time when the personal ads in the classified section of the newspaper was a big thing. We had some fun and created personal ads for our two brands of paint, Benjamin Moore and Martin Senour. We ran about six different ads every day for a week. On the right, you'll see a selection of them.

PERSONAL ADS.

Hi! My name is Benjamin Moore. I'm looking for someone to move in with. I'm a long term kind of guy who'll stick to your walls for many years. 775-1466.

Single gallon looking for married couple. If you're into a little roll on the walls call me. Martin Senour, 775-1466 days.

Hi, my name is Benjamin Moore. I've just moved in to a new place down the street and am anxious to make new friends. Call me at 775-1466 between 7:30 am and 4:30 pm.

Handsome guy who goes by the name of Martin Senour looking for handy woman to share colorful moments with. I'm 2 feet tall, and weight about 50 lbs. A lot of people say I look like a 5 gallon bucket of paint. Call 775-1466.

Tough guy by the name of Vulkem looking for a mature roof with leaks. I think we can bond together and solve your problems. My number is 775-1466.

Are you in the red? Call Benjamin Moore or Martin Senour. With the rates we charge, we'll have you in the pink in no time. Call 775-1466 any day except Sunday.

Are you blue? Call Martin Senour. I can help you change the mood of your room very easily. Call 775-1466.

Looking for someone to share apartment with. I can add so much color and excitement. Call Benjamin Moore at 775-1466.

Did someone give you the brush? Then I'm just the one for you. I'm a single gallon, of mixed color who'd like to spread himself on your walls. Call Martin Senour days at 775-1466.

Do you see everything as black or white? Then call Martin Senour or Benjamin Moore. We can help you see in over 5,000 different colors. Call 775-1466.

Anyone knowing the where-abouts of the person who keeps answering the phone with the word "Yellow!", please call Martin

Senour or Benjamin Moore at 775-1466. We want to hire them.

Single gallon looking for woman with a brush. Let's get together and paint the town red. Call Martin Senour at 775-1466.

Seeking married woman who wants a colorful affair in her home. You pick the color and I'll brighten your life. Call Benjamin Moore at 775-1466.

Are you green with envy? I can change your color mood. Call Martin Senour at 775-1466.

Looking for single, handy woman to watch movies with. My favorite

films are "The Color Purple", "Blue Yonder", "Soylent Green", "Black Rain" and "Fried Green Tomatoes". Call Benjamin Moore and lets start a colorful relationship. 775-1466.

How would you like to get togeth-er with six cute numbers? Then here they are: 7, 7, (they're twins), 5, 1, 4 and another set of twins , 6 and 6. Put them together on your phone and they'll show you a very colorful time.

Strong, silent type wishes to meet someone who needs protection from the outdoor elements. Call 775-1466 and ask for Vulkem.

Every girl deserves a new coat, even in the tropics. Call Martin Senour and he'll lay his coat on any surface in your home. 775-1466. Now, isn't that gallant?

ing. Call Benjamin Moore at 775-1466 and let's do it on your walls!

Anyone knowing the whereabouts of Benjamin Moore a.k.a. Ben 'Jammin' Moore, please call 775-1466.

Multi Colortural guys looking for open minded people to share paint stories. Call Benjamin Moore or Martin Senour at 775-1466.

Hi, my name is Martin Senour. I'm looking for someone who would like to watch my favorite TV show, C.S.I. (Coating Scene Investigation) with. Call 775-1466.

Looking for adventurous couple into sponging, stippling, smoosh-

AD NAUSEAM.

I've read that people are getting very good at looking at the internet and not seeing the ads. Advertising aversion.

They can consciously read the story and no matter how many little distractions there are on the screen, they just don't see them. I'm sure this is the same for print ads in newspapers.

But, have a look a this editorial spread with just one ad on it. The odds of getting noticed is going to be pretty good.

Because our ads are always surrounded by live editorial, I try to predict events and tie in the ad copy. Sometimes it works really well.

Earl becomes season's second hurricane

Wednesday, September 7, 2022   VIRGIN ISLANDS   The Virgin Islands Daily News   **3**

VITEMA tracking disturbances, new COVID vaccines available

By SUZANNE CARLSON
Daily News Staff

Virgin Islanders marked the fifth anniversary of Hurricane Irma's landfall in the territory on Tuesday, and officials said at the weekly Government House press briefing that there are no immediate threats of another storm approaching.

Tropical Storm Earl dumped heavy rain across the territory throughout the Labor Day weekend and into Tuesday, but V.I. Territorial Emergency Management Agency Director Daryl Jaschen said the storm was moving away from the Virgin Islands.

"There are no watches or warnings for the U.S. Virgin Islands at this time," Jaschen said.

Lightning and scattered thunderstorms are expected to continue through the week, and "strong thunderstorm squalls are also likely over local waters. If lightning is nearby, please seek shelter," Jaschen said.

The heat index is forecast to be over 100 degrees in urban coastal areas on Puerto Rico and St. Croix, Jaschen said.

Maritime conditions have been gradually improving after the rough weekend, but thunderstorms could cause potentially choppy conditions and boaters and beachgoers are urged to be cautious of wind gusts and rip currents, Jaschen said.

The heavy rains have left the ground saturated and prone to possible flooding, he added.

Jaschen said officials are monitoring two new disturbances forming off the west coast of Africa, and conditions could be conducive to some development as the systems move west, but the likelihood of further formation is low to medium over the next several days.

COVID-19 update

There are currently 203 active

Esther Ellis

> **Anyone age 12 and over is eligible to receive the Pfizer vaccine, and anyone 18 and older is eligible to receive the Moderna vaccine if it has been at least two months since your primary vaccine series.**

COVID-19 cases territory-wide, including 116 on St. Croix, 86 on St. Thomas, and one on St. John, according to Territorial Epidemiologist Dr. Esther Ellis.

Four COVID-19 patients are being treated at Schneider Hospital on St. Thomas, and five COVID-19 patients are at Luis Hospital on St. Croix.

Ellis said that bivalent COVID-19 vaccines, the new formulation that is more effective against the latest variants, is now available at Health Department clinics. There are 800 doses available territory-wide, including 600 from Pfizer and 200 from Moderna.

Anyone age 12 and over is eligible to receive the Pfizer vaccine, and anyone 18 and older is eligible to receive the Moderna vaccine if it has been at least two months since your primary vaccine series, Ellis said. The bivalent vaccine can also be used as a booster dose.

COVID testing is being conducted Monday through Friday from 9:30 a.m. to 10:30 a.m. at the Charles Harwood Memorial parking lot on St. Croix; Monday, Tuesday, Thursday and Friday from 9:30 to 10:30 a.m. at the Schneider Hospital loading dock on St. Thomas; and Wednesday from 12 to 3 p.m. on St. John.

The Federal Emergency Management Agency is still providing funding through a Funeral Assistance Program for all COVID-19 related deaths. The program is part of the Coronavirus Response and Relief Act of 2021 and the American Rescue Plan Act, and the Health Depart-

ment has been reaching out to family members of individuals who died from COVID-19, Ellis said. Affected families are also encouraged to apply for funeral assistance by contacting Lorraine Benjamin-Matthew, director of Vital Records and Statistics, at Lorraine.benjamin-matthew@doh.vi.gov, or call 340-474-9749.

Ellis said there are no confirmed cases of monkeypox in the territory, "which is great news."

Community Business Forum

The Office of the Governor, in partnership with Royal Caribbean Cruise Line and the Department of Tourism, is holding its fifth USVI Community Business Forum to prepare for the upcoming cruising season from 9 to 11 a.m., on Thursday, Sept. 8, at the University of the Virgin Islands Great Hall on St. Croix.

For more information and to register for the free forum, visit vi.gov/cbf.

— Contact Suzanne Carlson at 340-714-9122 or email scarlson@dailynews.vi.

Port Hamilton addresses ownership, refinery restart in letter to senators

By SUZANNE CARLSON
Daily News Staff

Port Hamilton Refining and Transportation sent a letter to the Legislature Monday, assuring senators that a fire smoldering for weeks at the St. Croix refinery was extinguished on Aug. 26, but company officials did not fully respond to the lawmakers' questions and concerns.

Fermin Rodriguez

"I am totally not satisfied with what I received," said Sen. Kenneth Gittens, chairman of the Committee on Economic Development and Agriculture.

The committee met on July 14 and senators questioned Port Hamilton officials about their plans to restart the refinery, and asked for more information about who owns the company.

Port Hamilton Principal Charles Chambers assured senators he would provide a list of owners and investors. But after he failed to do so, Gittens sent Chambers a letter on Aug. 26, listing specific information for the company to provide by Sept. 5.

While the company met the deadline, Gittens said he is disappointed in the response.

"What I'll be doing next is working with our colleagues to see our way forward, what will be next," Gittens said.

He also plans to consult with the Legislature's chief legal counsel, as "the people of the Virgin Islands demand answers and they should be able to get them."

The Aug. 26 letter requested several pieces of information, including an update on a pile of petroleum coke fuel that began smoldering on Aug. 4 at the refinery on Aug. 4.

For weeks, the company, for weeks, said the smoldering coke was under control and crews were dousing the fuel with water 24-hours a day. But on Aug. 21, a fire broke out "within the petroleum coke conveyor loading system located outside and above the Coke Storage Dome," according to a press release issued by refinery manager Fermin Rodriguez, which noted that one firefighter suffered a minor burn.

The company has not issued any subsequent public statements since the fire began, and has not responded to any questions from The Daily News.

Gittens said the company responded late Monday evening, and he provided a copy of the two-page letter from Rodriguez.

The letter begins by noting that the "smoldering coke discovered on August 4, 2022" was "completely extinguished by Friday, August 26."

"Port Hamilton provided the resources and personnel in connection with the smoldering coke. The process used to accomplish this was to first saturate the coke with water, then to remove part of the material in the dome to make room for heavy equipment to alternatively spread the coke pile and apply water to cool the coke," according to the letter.

The coke was leftover from a brief but disastrous restart under former owner Limetree Bay Refining, which sprayed oil and noxious gas over neighborhoods around the refinery before the Environmental Protection Agency issued an emergency shutdown order in 2021.

Limetree Bay entered bankruptcy and did not have the cash available to complete cleanup and shutdown of the refinery before it was transferred to Port Hamilton.

Port Hamilton has been operating five offsite air monitoring stations throughout the "smoldering coke event, and no adverse impacts were recorded," according to the letter from Rodriguez.

He noted that officials from the Department of Planning and Natural Resources and the EPA have visited the site and "no further actions have been requested from these agencies."

"At present Port Hamilton is in the process of analyzing the coke for future transportation off island," Fermin said, thanking staff, contractors and emergency personnel who worked to resolve the issue. "Port Hamilton wishes to acknowledge the work performed by all its employees, contractors and emergency personnel that responded to this event and worked expeditiously and safely to resolve this issue."

In regard to the questions posed during the July 14 hearing, Rodriguez confirmed that Port Hamilton is a limited liability limited partnership that acquired the title to the refinery assets in January following the Limetree Bay bankruptcy auction.

"Consistent with the requirements of the Virgin Islands Code, Port Hamilton has disclosed that Virgin Islands Refining Co., LLC, is its general partner. Local counsel has confirmed that there is no statutory requirement for Port Hamilton to disclose its limited partners. Further, Port Hamilton has entered into Confidentiality and Non-Disclosure Agreements which require that Port Hamilton not disclose its limited partners," according to the letter.

That contradicts statements Chambers made during the July 14 hearing.

Back at the July hearing, when senators pressed Chambers to provide a list of other owners and investors in the refinery prior to adjournment, Chambers said he didn't have the list available.

Gittens asked Chambers: "The list that we asked for, were you able to get it?"

Monday's letter also assured senators that Port Hamilton is providing DPNR and the EPA with weekly updates, and "EPA has direct access to live, instantaneous air monitoring data. Port Hamilton is also working with DPNR to provide them with similar access to air monitoring data.

"In addition, Port Hamilton has had several meetings with EPA and DPNR to address questions from the Government. Port Hamilton has been responsive to the EPA regarding any comments in connection with re-starting the refinery, and Port Hamilton will continue to do so," according to the statement.

Further, Port Hamilton is still preparing to restart the refinery, and "is in the process of reviewing all safety, health, environmental and process operations procedures to ensure safe and environmentally compliant operations."

Rodriguez also provided an update on efforts to place additional air monitoring stations around the refinery, and listed three phases of their refinery restart plan.

Phase 1 involves "topping," and "startup of the No 5 Crude and corresponding equipment," Phase 2 involves hydro-skimming, and phase 3 involves startup of the Coker unit for "Heavy Oil operation," but the company has not identified a startup date for any of the phases, according to the letter.

— Contact Suzanne Carlson at 340-714-9122 or email scarlson@dailynews.vi.

2 The Virgin Islands Daily News   VIRGIN ISLANDS   Monday, January 10, 2022

'Grim reality': Could Ghislaine Maxwell flip on others now that she's convicted?

By BEN WIEDER and JULIE K. BROWN
Miami Herald

NEW YORK — Ghislaine Maxwell will likely spend the rest of her life in prison unless she can win an appeal — or is willing to come clean about everyone who was involved in Jeffrey Epstein's criminal enterprise.

Even then, experts say it will depend on what she knows and when the crimes happened.

Maxwell's conviction Dec. 29 on five of six sex charges was a stunning denouement for the former British socialite who counted royalty, presidents and some of the world's wealthiest people among her closest friends. It also presents the possibility that she could be sentenced to decades in prison, largely because she was found guilty of sex trafficking a minor, the most serious charge — which carries a maximum penalty of 40 years.

Still, for survivors, punishing Epstein's top lieutenant is not enough. They say, Maxwell, Epstein's longtime girlfriend, recruited underage girls to be sexually abused by the multimillionaire. And that she had help.

"Maxwell did not act alone. Others must be held accountable. I have faith that they will be," said Virginia Giuffre, who was recruited by Maxwell when she was 16 and successfully sued Maxwell in 2016.

Prosecutors said that Maxwell had recruited and groomed four girls, two as young as 14 when they first met Maxwell, to be abused by Epstein, the financier, who had sumptuous homes in Florida, Manhattan and New Mexico, and who owned two private islands in the U.S. Virgin Islands. He died in federal custody in August 2019 in what has been ruled a suicide, one month after he was arrested on sex trafficking charges.

Now the question that everyone is asking is whether Maxwell, 60, will name names of others who helped Epstein — or some of their friends who may have participated in the abuse of girls and young women.

The problem, however, is whether the crimes are even prosecutable, experts say.

Prince Andrew, left, with his arm around Virginia Roberts Giuffre, then 17, who claims she was paid by Jeffrey Epstein to have sex with the prince. On the right is Ghislaine Maxwell.
Photo from U.S. DISTRICT COURT SOUTHERN DISTRICT OF NEW YORK

> "Maxwell did not act alone. Others must be held accountable. I have faith that they will be."
> — Virginia Roberts Giuffre

"The statute of limitations for these crimes are probably long past. But if she knows of new crimes — depending on the nature of the allegations and the victims — the government is likely to consider it," said former federal prosecutor Paul Pelletier, who worked in the Justice Department for nearly 30 years.

"She could talk about the parties on the islands — but the question is whether any of it is within the [statute of] limitation period. She was with him for many years after that, so if he or others did commit any crimes against women, she would be the one to know."

Maxwell's family indicated that she is innocent and is planning to appeal her conviction.

"We believe firmly in our sister's innocence — we are very disappointed with the verdict. We have already started the appeal tonight and we believe that she will ultimately be vindicated," her family said in a statement.

David S. Weinstein, a former assistant U.S. attorney in the Southern District of Florida, said he sees any potential appeal is unlikely to succeed. The fact that one of the six charges was returned not guilty, for example, would make it hard for Maxwell's lawyers to argue that the jury was pressured to deliver a verdict, even though the judge had urged jurors to deliberate longer each day to stave off the possibility of a mistrial should one of them contract COVID-19.

Federal prosecutors and Maxwell confirmed

See **MAXWELL***, page 4*

WE KNOW WHAT YOU DID IN YOUR BEDROOM!

THE PAINT DEPOT
ST. THOMAS, V.I.
775-1466

We also know what you did in your closet, kitchen and living room. You see, when you choose a custom tinted Benjamin Moore paint from us, we make up a file card with our name, the type of paint used, the color formula, even what room you used it in. It's great when you need to come back and get touch up paint in the future. And don't worry, we're very discreet. We would never tell a soul what you did in any of your rooms.

Benjamin Moore, Martin Senour, Pratt & Lambert and Zinsser PermaWhite paints; Vulkem, ToughKote & Silicone roof coatings. PLUS the best service anywhere!

TIMING AND LUCK.

Sometimes, timing and luck is with you and your ad headline is an extension of the big editorial story. Like when the Jeffrey Epstein scandal story was all over the news.

Everyone in the Virgin Islands knew about Epstein as he owned Little St. James, a small island close to St. Thomas.

So when we ran the ad with this headline, "We Know What You Did In Your Bedroom!" surrounded by a story about Epstein, Prince Andrew and Ghislaine Maxwell, you just know people were going to read that ad.

182

THE CARNIVAL WAS OVER.

The Annual Carnival was over and I knew they'd have a big editorial on it that Monday. So we ran our "Don't Stop The Carnival" ad.

This headline is also the title of the Herman Wouk novel which takes place in a fictional Caribbean island but was really in St. Thomas. He lived there for a while.

Members of The Gypsies Troupe portrayed masqueraders as they made their way down Main Street for the 2023 Adults' Parade on Saturday.

Adults' Parade with color, pageantry was 'mas for the ages'

By KIT MACAVOY
Daily News Staff

ST. THOMAS — Defying a few gray clouds and early morning rain showers, lead cars bearing Carnival royalty shifted into drive and cruised down Kronprindsens Gade just before noon on Saturday. In their wake, steel bands played, troupes tramped and spectators lining the streets drank in the sights and sounds of the 2023 Adults' Parade.

Before the troupes took their first steps, and amid the warm-up riffs of eager steel drummers, Tamra Olive, Virgin Islands Judicial Branch Pretrial Intervention director, said the Superior Court Rising Stars Youth Steel Orchestra would perform a series of local songs, medleys and some songs from Trinidad.

Started in 1984 by then Chief Territorial Court Judge Verne A. Hodge, the group aims to prevent juvenile delinquency and school dropout among the territory's youth.

"Because of COVID, we didn't get to recruit for two years," she said. "So we recruited last summer. So we have a lot of fresh new kids and then we have like 26 graduating members this year, so we're recruiting again."

One of those seniors, Cherae Frett, 17, said she was looking forward to seeing people enjoy music, colorful costumes and dancing.

The Rising Stars program gives kids "a place to go after school and stay out of trouble," she said. After she graduates, Frett said she'll be back to work at the summer camp and help mentor the next generation of rising stars.

Longtime troupe, The Jesters, took the lead as the first to follow the pageant winners on the route that went past Emancipation Garden to Lionel Roberts Stadium in Hospital Ground.

"We make our own clothing, our own headpieces," said Jesters Costume Chair Laverne C. Blyden. It was the troupe's 37th year at the parade.

"And actually, our signature is our headpieces." Jesters seamstress Celita Smith added, and referencing the sparkling anchor adorning the caps of each troupe member.

Spectacular familiars followed as other well-known troupes like the Eagles, Elskoe and Associates, Hugga Bunch, Infernos and Gypsies performed in feathered splendor down the road past enthusiastic paradegoers, stopping along the way to take pictures with fans.

Among the other groups were Xtasy, Whatahparty, Ultimate Legacy and Remedy, the latter boasting

See **PARADE**, page 3

DON'T STOP THE CARNIVAL!

It's still on at The Paint Depot! Our colorful troop of paint mixers will dazzle you as they tramp down the aisles, whip that gallon in the tint machine and then spin it round and round to get your perfect color.

You are, of course, welcome to dance by the cash register as your paint is getting ready.

Benjamin Moore, Pratt & Lambert and Zinsser PermaWhite paints; Vulkem, ToughKote & GE Silicone roof coatings. PLUS the best service anywhere!

THE PAINT DEPOT
ST. THOMAS, V.I.
775-1466

2 The Virgin Islands Daily News
VIRGIN ISLANDS
Monday, December 19, 2022

TSK's Christmas serenade coming to neighborhoods east and west

By FIONA STOKES
Special to the Daily News

ST. CROIX — The sights, sounds and smells of the holiday season abound, but on St. Croix in particular, it isn't quite Christmas without 'Stanley and dem'.

Formally known as Stanley and the Ten Sleepless Knights or TSK, the scratch band has had residents literally dancing in their Christmas pajamas at wee morning hours, as their flatbed truck carrying huge speakers slowly makes its way through neighborhood streets, east and west.

It's become an annual tradition for the group to serenade at Christmas with old-time carols — some set to quelbe tunes. The tradition stopped in 1992 after a few grinches complained about "noise." The serenade was revived about a decade ago when WTJX — under the leadership of Osbert Potter — set out to film a documentary on the group with assistance from St. Croix Avis owner Rena Brodhurst.

During Festival season, TSK is almost always called upon to spread love and Christmas cheer throughout the community, but the serenade is by far one of the favorite events many look forward to. Now mostly made up of beloved octogenarians, TSK has added a few newcomers including Kendall Henry.

One of the younger members of the band, Henry said the serenade is an important part of local culture because it keeps the traditions of quelbe music alive as it was done years ago. He said the event — which includes a motorcade, food stops and tramp — had to be curtailed over the last two years because of COVID-19 restrictions, but this year a full-scale event is in store for residents.

This year, there will be two nights of live music and two additional nights of pre-recorded music when the flatbed truck that carries the band will drive through neighborhoods that they usually do not get to.

"It's because of time and with all the speakers on the large truck it is hard to get to some of the surrounding neighborhoods, but we wanted to get to them too, so we added some nights and the band will go through — but with prerecorded music and not all the instruments and equipment," Henry said.

The truck and the throngs of revelers — by foot and by car — enjoying the music will meet up with others at "food stops "with traditional Crucian cuisine in Ginger Thomas and Estate Grove Place on the second night and Estate St. John and Eliza's Retreat on the fourth night."

This year the serenade series, with pre-recorded music, will kick off beginning at 7 p.m. Tuesday in Ginger Thomas at the Christian residence. It will make its way east, through Christiansted and back. The serenade will continue just after midnight Wednesday morning with live music — again starting in Ginger Thomas and winding its way through Strawberry, Bonne Esperance, Mon Bijou, Calquohoun, Grove Place, Whim, Campo Rico and into Frederiksted town. Once in town, a tramp will begin at the Frederiksted post office and down King Street into the Midre Cummings Park where the traditional Crucian Breakfast will be held.

On Thursday, the truck with pre-recorded music will leave Ginger Thomas, but this time wind its way west. Then at midnight on Friday, live music will abound with TSK atop its flatbed truck, winding their way through Peter's Rest, Anna's Hope, Orange Grove, Golden Rock, Harbor View, La Grande Princesse, Estate St. John, Christiansted town, Eliza's Retreat, Tide Village and back to town. A tramp will follow, beginning at 6 a.m. at Sunday Market Square, heading to the WTJX building in Estate Richmond where breakfast will be served.

For those unfamiliar with the term Crucian breakfast or traditional Crucian cuisine, the spread at each stop is expected to include everything from stewed saltfish, pick-up saltfish also known as saltfish gundee, smoke herring, boiled eggs, spinach, okra, kallaloo, souse, fresh baked titi or butter bread, banana fritters, goat water and other soups, Johnny cake, oatmeal, cream of wheat, bush tea, and cocoa tea among others.

Residents who want to donate dishes or drinks to the Crucian Breakfast events, or guavaberry rum and other goodies for the band, should contact Henry at 1(210) 867-4913 or Tanya Singh at WTJX at 340-718-3339.

Stanley and the Ten Sleepless Knights entertain during the 2019 Christmas morning serenade. *Daily News file photo*

I'M DREAMING OF A... THE PAINT DEPOT

...white Christmas,
red Christmas,
blue Christmas,
yellow Christmas,
or any other color you can think of Christmas!
Have it any way you want with Benjamin Moore quality paints.

ST. THOMAS, V.I.
775-1466

Benjamin Moore, Pratt & Lambert and Zinsser PermaWhite paints; Vulkem, TougKote & GE Silicone roof coatings. PLUS the best service anywhere!

MORE WELL TIMED ADS.

Great timing again for Christmas ad and election ad on right.

I get lucky with about a dozen ads a year that work seamlessly with the editorial.

184

Trump seeks White House again amid GOP losses, legal probes

By JILL COLVIN
The Associated Press

PALM BEACH, Fla. — Former President Donald Trump said Tuesday that he will mount a third White House campaign, launching an early start to the 2024 contest. The announcement comes just a week after an underwhelming midterm showing for Republicans and will force the party to decide whether to embrace a candidate whose refusal to accept defeat in 2020 pushed American democracy to the brink.

"I am tonight announcing my candidacy for president of the United States," Trump said to an audience of several hundred supporters, club members and gathered press in a chandeliered ballroom at his Mar-a-Lago club, where he stood flanked by more than 30 American flags and banners that read, "MAKE AMERICA GREAT AGAIN!"

Trump enters the race in a moment of political vulnerability. He hoped to launch his campaign in the wake of resounding GOP midterm victories, fueled by candidates he elevated during this year's primaries. Instead, many of those candidates lost, allowing Democrats to keep the Senate and leaving the GOP with a path to only a bare majority in the House.

Far from the undisputed leader of the party, Trump is now facing criticism from some of his own allies, who say it's time for Republicans to look to the future, with Florida Gov. Ron DeSantis emerging as an early favorite White

Former President Donald Trump arrives to speak at Mar-a-Lago on Election Day, Nov. 8, in Palm Beach, Fla.
File photo by ASSOCIATED PRESS

House contender.

The former president is still popular with the GOP base. But other Republicans, including former Vice President Mike Pence, are taking increasingly public steps toward campaigns of their own, raising the prospect that Trump will have to navigate a competitive GOP primary.

He's launching his candidacy amid a series of escalating criminal investigations, including several that could lead to indictments. They include the probe into dozens of documents with classified markings that were seized by the FBI from Mar-a-Lago and ongoing state and federal inquiries into his efforts to overturn the results of the 2020 presidential election.

Another campaign is a remarkable turn for any former president, much less one who made history as the first to be impeached twice and whose term ended with his supporters violently storming the Capitol in a deadly bid to halt the peaceful transition of power on Jan. 6, 2021.

But Trump, according to people close to him, has been eager to return to politics and try to halt the rise of other potential challengers. Aides have spent the last months readying paperwork, identifying potential staff and sketching out the contours of a campaign that is being modeled on his 2016 operation, when a small clutch of aides zipping between rallies on his private jet defied the odds and defeated far better-funded and more experienced rivals by tapping into deep political fault lines and using shocking statements to drive relentless media attention.

Even after GOP losses, Trump remains the most powerful force in his party. For years he has consistently topped his fellow Republican contenders by wide margins in hypothetical head-to-head matchups. And even out of office, he consistently attracts thousands to his rallies and remains his party's most prolific fundraiser, raising hundreds of millions of dollars.

But Trump is also a deeply polarizing figure. Fifty-four percent of voters in last week's midterm elections viewed him very or somewhat unfavorably, according to AP VoteCast, a survey of more than 94,000 voters nationwide. And an October AP-NORC poll found even Republicans have their reservations about him remaining the party's standard-bearer, with 43% saying they don't want to see him run for president in 2024.

While some Republicans with presidential ambitions, like former U.N. Ambassador Nikki Haley, have long ruled out running against Trump, others have said he would not figure into their decisions, even before his midterm losses.

They include Pence, who released a book Tuesday, and Trump's former secretary of state, Mike Pompeo, as well as former New Jersey Gov. Chris Christie, who ran against Trump in 2016.

But the person who has most occupied Trump and his allies in recent months is DeSantis, whose commanding reelection as governor last week was a bright spot for Republicans this cycle. The former congressman, who became a popular national figure among conservatives during the pandemic as he pushed back on COVID-19 restrictions, shares Trump's pugilistic instincts and has embraced fights over social issues with similar zeal.

Even some enthusiastic Trump supporters say they are eager for DeSantis to run, seeing him as a natural successor to Trump but without the former president's considerable baggage.

Trump has already begun to lash out at DeSantis publicly. On Tuesday, the Florida governor shot back.

"At the end of the day, I would just tell people to go check out the scoreboard from last Tuesday night," DeSantis told reporters.

Public Works: candidates must remove political signs or face a fine

Daily News Staff

The Public Works Department announced Tuesday that candidates with political signs on either public or private property must be removed by early December of face a fine.

According to a released statement, the signage includes the posts or frames on which they were placed — all of whichmust be removed by Dec. 6.

The department "understood the need for candidates to reach voters through roadside signage, however, with elections over, all political signs — on public or private property — must be removed from roadsides," the release stated.

If the signs are not removed by Dec. 6, Public Works will remove them for a $150 fee, per sign.

"The sign owner will be unable to retrieve said signs unless payment is made in full. If signs are not collected within 30 days after removal, they will be discarded. Future permitting will be impacted for violators," the release stated.

According to the statement, it's the responsibility of each candidate or campaign organization to comply with the department's rules regarding removal of any signs on the roadside.

Residents who come across political signs after Dec. 6 can take a photo and email it to: notices@dailynews.vi.

REPUBLICANS & DEMOCRATS HAVE ALWAYS AGREED ON ONE THING…

…that The Paint Depot is THE place to buy paint and roof coatings. Come in anytime and experience politically correct service, liberal prices and conservative product values.

THE PAINT DEPOT
ST. THOMAS, V.I.
775-1466

Benjamin Moore, Pratt & Lambert and Zinsser PermaWhite paints, Vulkem, ToughKote and GE Silicone roof coatings. PLUS the best service anywhere!

MILDEW.

minority in the Virgin Islands.

Living in the Caribbean, humidity is always there. And when you have humidity, there's a good chance of having mildew in your home especially since air conditioned homes are in the

JUST SAY NO TO MILDEW.

Our Zinsser PermaWhite paint is just what you need if you live high up in mildew country. Why? Because Zinsser PermaWhite paint comes with a 5 year manufacturer warranty against mildew. So come down from up there and visit us down here.

THE PAINT DEPOT

Coatings for every surface from the most knowledgeable and service oriented paint people.
AT THE TOP OF RAPHUNE HILL, ST. THOMAS, VIRGIN ISLANDS. 775-1466

MORE AND MORE
I THINK ABOUT MILDEW
LESS AND LESS

That's because I used Zinsser PermaWhite mildew proof paint in my house.

Applied like any household paint, PermaWhite is guaranteed to prevent mildew growth for 5 years when two coats are applied according to label directions. (The first coat primes and seals the surface; the second coat provides mildew and moisture resistance.) It's also extremely durable.

So, if you want to think about mildew less and less, you'll need to think about Zinsser PermaWhite more and more.

THE PAINT DEPOT
Coatings for every surface from the most knowledgeable and service oriented paint people.
AT THE TOP OF RAPHUNE HILL, ST. THOMAS, VIRGIN ISLANDS. 775-1466

Title: 'Primer and Two Coats'
Medium: 100% acrylic latex paint on canvas. 24" x 30"
Artist: Ben 'Jammin' Moore
Paint: B-M Regal premium interior satin
Color: 'Tricycle Red'
Price: .23 cents a square foot, includes warranty
Viewing: Mon-Fri: 7:30am to 4:30pm; Sat: 7:30 am to 2 pm.

When you invest in paint for your home,
deal with the professionals who know more about coatings
than anyone else in the Virgin Islands.

THE PAINT DEPOT
Coatings for every surface from the most knowledgeable and service oriented paint people.
AT THE TOP OF RAPHUNE HILL, ST. THOMAS, VIRGIN ISLANDS. 775-1466

FITTING THE MESSAGE TO THE MEDIUM.

Whenever possible, it's important to tie in your ad to the audience.

For the Humane Society booklet, we ran the ad with the headline "Down boy, DOWN!" which you can see in the introduction to this book. The ad on the left ran in an Arts Alive, a art oriented magazine. It ran in color with the frame in gold and the inside bright red.

The ad on the right ran in the high school fund raising booklet.

THE FINE PRINT OF LIFE

"Half of getting what you want
is knowing what you must first give up
in order to achieve it."

From your supporters at

THE PAINT DEPOT

Coatings for every surface from the most knowledgeable and service oriented paint people.
AT THE TOP OF RAPHUNE HILL, ST. THOMAS, VIRGIN ISLANDS. 775-1466

RALPH LAUREN
SPECIALIZED PAINTS.

Here are four ads we ran to promote
Ralph Lauren paints.

FREE FEEL.

Imagine a paint that not only looks like linen or suede or river rocks but actually *feels* like linen and suede and river rocks.
With Ralph Lauren Designer paint finishes that's what you get. We also have Ralph Lauren technique tools to make your
walls look like fine aged leather, denim, chambray or crackled paint.
So come in and don't just look at the paint, get a feel for our newest paints from Ralph Lauren.

THE PAINT DEPOT

Coatings for every surface from the most knowledgeable and service oriented paint people.
AT THE TOP OF RAPHUNE HILL, ST. THOMAS, VIRGIN ISLANDS. 775-1466

Our paint suppliers have coop advertising dollars where they'll pay 50% of the cost of the ad. However, you'd have to run their ads with all their rules. And that would have meant boring ads. So, we just did our thing.

I'LL SHOW YOU MINE.

If you come in to the store, I'll show you mine...my walls, that is. You see, I did up my office using Pratt & Lambert's Ovation suede finish paint. Wow! It really has the look and feel of brushed suede. And the best thing about it is, it's very easy to do. Come in and I'll show you how.
And once you're finished painting your own suede finished walls, you can invite me over to show me yours.

THE PAINT DEPOT

Coatings for every surface from the most knowledgeable and service oriented paint people.
AT THE TOP OF RAPHUNE HILL, ST. THOMAS, VIRGIN ISLANDS. 775-1466

30% OFF ALL RALPH LAUREN COATS!

Paint coats that is. Get 30% off in stock Ralph Lauren paints.
Hurry!

THE PAINT DEPOT

Coatings for every surface from the most knowledgeable and service oriented paint people.
AT THE TOP OF RAPHUNE HILL, ST. THOMAS, VIRGIN ISLANDS. 775-1466

WALLPAPER IN A PAINT CAN.

If you're looking for a paint that not only looks like linen but actually feels like linen then come in and check out our newest paint line, Ralph Lauren Designer paints. We can also make your walls look like fine, aged leather, a denim jacket, a chambray shirt or crackled paint. How about suede or river rocks? Come in and don't just look at the paint, get a feel for it with Ralph Lauren.

THE PAINT DEPOT

Coatings for every surface from the most knowledgeable and service oriented paint people.

AT THE TOP OF RAPHUNE HILL, ST. THOMAS, VIRGIN ISLANDS. 775-1466

HOW MUCH PAINT IS IN A GALLON OF PAINT?

This is not a trick question. You see, some paints have more water in each gallon and less 'guts'.
Take Benjamin-Moore's Moorlife exterior latex paint for example. It has less water in each gallon than other leading brands.
More 'guts', less water means better coverage in one coat and a longer lasting paint on your walls.
So if you want more paint in each gallon of paint,
ask for Benjamin-Moore Moorlife paint.

THE PAINT DEPOT

Coatings for every surface from the most knowledgeable and service oriented paint people.
AT THE TOP OF RAPHUNE HILL, ST. THOMAS, VIRGIN ISLANDS. 775-1466

Yes, we really do have an employee whose last name is Aitken.

THE AITKEN DIET.

Kirsty Aitken, our Office Manager,
has come up with a great way to lose extra calories.
Here it is:

Scrape exterior of house: 350 calories
Power wash exterior of house: 150 calories
Apply one coat of Zinsser 123 primer: 200 calories
Apply two coats of Great Life exterior satin paint: 400 calories
Total calories lost: 1,100.

Now, both you *and* your house will get envious looks.

THE PAINT DEPOT

Coatings for every surface from the most knowledgeable and service oriented paint people.
AT THE TOP OF RAPHUNE HILL, ST. THOMAS, VIRGIN ISLANDS. 775-1466

HAVE YOU EVER HEARD THE SOUND A NEW PAINT COLOR MAKES?

I don't know about you, but getting me to paint a room in our house requires a lot of diplomacy on my wife's part.
But once done, the sound of that new paint color is music to my ears.
("Honey, that color looks beautiful! You did such a great job. Did you get a sore neck painting?
Come here and I'll give you a little neck rub. You're such a sweetie! Thanks a million!")
We have over 5000 Benjamin Moore and Martin Senour colors you can try out.
Each one makes a completely different sound.

THE PAINT DEPOT

Coatings for every surface from the most knowledgeable and service oriented paint people.
AT THE TOP OF RAPHUNE HILL, ST. THOMAS, VIRGIN ISLANDS. 775-1466

BLING! BLING!

Looking to add richness on your lamps, walls or other knick knacks? Then try our gold, silver, bronze and copper metallic latex glazes by Benjamin Moore. Truly stunning effects right out of the can.

THE PAINT DEPOT

Coatings for every surface from the most knowledgeable and service oriented paint people.

AT THE TOP OF RAPHUNE HILL, ST. THOMAS, VIRGIN ISLANDS. 775-1466

IDLE HANDS ARE THE DEVIL'S WORKSHOP!

Boy, have we got the perfect thing to keep you out of trouble...paint your bedroom this weekend! We have over 5,000 tempting colors to choose from including 'Heavenly Blue' and 'Heavens to Betsy'. And the cost? Two gallons of Martin-Senour Proline Premium interior latex semi-gloss, white or pastel, will run you $26.54. Add a decent 2" cutting brush, one 1/2" sleeve, one heavy duty roller frame and a sturdy plastic paint tray and you're at $37.67 total. A sinfully small price to pay to have your mate treat you like an angel.

THE PAINT DEPOT

Coatings for every surface from the most knowledgeable and service oriented paint people.
AT THE TOP OF RAPHUNE HILL, ST. THOMAS, VIRGIN ISLANDS. 775-1466

The expression "it was as slow as watching paint dry" got me searching the internet and finding a site that shows paint drying. Again, a tidbit that turned into an ad. I don't know if that paint drying site is still up today.

WATCHING PAINT DRY.

If you'd like to see how paint dries, go to this website and you'll see an animated version of what actually happens to paint when it dries. It's really exciting. Well, for us it is.
(www.polymercentre.org.uk/community/features/emulsion.php)
Now, if you're into watching real paint dry on real walls, the best to watch is Benjamin Moore paint. That's because their colors are chosen by more interior designers than any other brand so it makes it much more pleasing and relaxing to the eye. And with over 3000 colors to pick from, you'll be up all night deciding which color you'll want to watch dry.

THE PAINT DEPOT

Coatings for every surface from the most knowledgeable and service oriented paint people.
AT THE TOP OF RAPHUNE HILL, ST. THOMAS, VIRGIN ISLANDS. 775-1466

"I'M SITTING IN THE SMALLEST ROOM OF MY HOUSE."

I'm a little claustrophobic, so I try not to spend too much time in there. Then I remembered, 'the right paint color can make the room seem bigger'. So, I called the people at The Paint Depot and they tell me that light colors will make the walls feel like they are further away, while dark colors bring the walls in. Well, I rushed out and got a quart of Benjamin Moore Regal Satin paint in a very pale blue color. (That's right, one quart. I told you this room was really small.) Now that I've finished painting my bathroom, the room didn't get physically bigger but the feeling of openness is definitely there. Now I'm sitting pretty.

THE PAINT DEPOT

Coatings for every surface from the most knowledgeable and service oriented paint people.
AT THE TOP OF RAPHUNE HILL, ST. THOMAS, VIRGIN ISLANDS. 775-1466

PAINT, IS PAINT, IS PAINT.

Open any can and look inside. They all look the same whether you pay $11.95, $19.95, or $35.95 a gallon.
But what you can't see is what separates the men from the boys (and the women from the girls).
The ingredients.
The better the paint, the more 'guts' in each gallon. It's what makes paint last longer, go on easier,
and hide better. We recommend the best paint for use outside in the harsh environment and a less expensive paint for inside.
But, whatever grade of paint you end up buying from us, you'll get this with every purchase:
incredible service from the most knowledgeable people in the paint business.
After all, every paint store looks the same until you get inside and check out the 'human ingredients'.

THE PAINT DEPOT

Coatings for every surface from the most knowledgeable and service oriented paint people.
AT THE TOP OF RAPHUNE HILL, ST. THOMAS, VIRGIN ISLANDS. 775-1466

THE HAND PUPPET AD. ANOTHER WAY TO PHYSICALLY ENGAGE THE READER.

Many years ago, when I worked as a promotion manager for a group of magazines, I created a direct mail piece to a select group of prospects. If I recall, the mailing was to about 300 people.

In that mailing, I used an actual hand puppet and a script was attached. It was very well received.

I couldn't do a mailing like this to 17,000 residents so I came up with this. I think parents, even if they were not interested in buying roof coating as this time, would have made the puppet for their kids.

The ad ran in the inside gutter of a double page spread.

One of only a handfull of 4-color ads I ever ran.

The PAINT DEPOT presents the one act play
"TOUGHKOTE ON A HOT TIN ROOF"

Instructions:
Cut out hand puppet on left page. Tape tabs together. Place hand in puppet. Follow script below.
(You might want to close your door. I mean, do you really want people to see what you're about to do?)

fade in:
You're reading an article about the heavy tropical rains that are going to be here until late November.
You're wondering what roof coating to use when all of a sudden, Rufus Coates walks up to you.

Rufus:
(with excitement)
Good morning! My name is Rufus Coates and I work at
The Paint Depot.

You:
(shaking hands with Rufus)
Pleased to meet you. What brings you here?

(dark forboding skies form outside)
Rufus:
Well, I was so excited about our ToughKote roof coating that
I decided to run over to talk to you.

You:
What's so exciting about roof coating?

Rufus:
Well, first of all, did you know that ToughKote roof coating
has the same NSF potable water testing as the "other" guy
and that it's thicker?

You:
(leaning forward on your desk, intent look)
No, I didn't know that.

Rufus:
Well, here comes the best part...*the very best part.*
ToughKote roof coating is on sale for about $30.00 less per
bucket than the "other" leading brand.

You:
(eyes and mouth wide open)
WOW! Now that's exciting news! I've got a 2000 sq. ft. roof
that needs recoating. How much money would I save using
ToughKote roof coating?

Rufus:
Based on rolling the stuff on at 100 sq. ft. per gallon, you'd
save $120.00

You:
That's a lot money to just leave up on my roof! By the way,
where are you guys at?

Rufus:
We're at the top of Raphune Hill. And if you need to call
The Paint Depot, the number is 775-1466.

You:
(jotting down the number)
Thanks a lot. I'm heading over now!

THE END

A QUART OF PREVENTION IS WORTH A GALLON OF CURE.

Here is something you need to have around the house that you don't even need a prescription for: a quart of "Rust Destroyer". This isn't just any metal primer but a patented rust converting primer engineered to keep rust away longer than other brands. So, when you see early signs of rust around your property, pull out your quart of Rust Destroyer, and prevent it from spreading. You'll be saving yourself gallons and gallons of work later.

THE PAINT DEPOT

Coatings for every surface from the most knowledgeable and service oriented paint people.
AT THE TOP OF RAPHUNE HILL, ST. THOMAS, VIRGIN ISLANDS. 775-1466

The doors of the Paint Depot are painted blue as well as the lettering of our name on the building.

RAP CITY IN BLUE.

Music has changed a lot since 'Rhapsody in Blue'. Even the name for the color blue has changed dramatically.
Use to be, blue was either light blue or dark blue. Nowadays, when choosing a blue paint color, you'll
see names like 'old blue jeans', 'yin yang', 'lazy sunday', 'crisp morning air', 'grandma's sweater'.
But one thing that hasn't changed since we opened our 'blue doors',
is the warm and helpful service you get from the people here.

THE PAINT DEPOT

Coatings for every surface from the most knowledgeable and service oriented paint people.
AT THE TOP OF RAPHUNE HILL, ST. THOMAS, VIRGIN ISLANDS. 775-1466

OFFICIAL SUPPLIER OF RAINBOWS TO THE VIRGIN ISLANDS.

It wasn't easy to negotiate a deal like this, but we did it.
The thing that clinched it for us was of course, color selection. Benjamin Moore paints are specified by
more architects and interior designers than any other brand of paint. And rightfully so!
So the next time you see a rainbow in the Virgin Islands, those are Benjamin Moore colors custom
mixed by the talented people right here at The Paint Depot.

THE PAINT DEPOT

Coatings for every surface from the most knowledgeable and service oriented paint people.
AT THE TOP OF RAPHUNE HILL, ST. THOMAS, VIRGIN ISLANDS. 775-1466

In addition to Vulkem roof coating products, we sell their crack and joint sealant.

WHAT ARE YOU DOING IN A JOINT LIKE THIS?

When it comes to sealing joints between concrete, wood or metal, nothing beats Vulkem sealants.
It's flexible, waterproof and has tremendous adhesion.
So, when it's time to waterproof and seal your joint, there's only one place to go to.
Our joint.

THE PAINT DEPOT

Coatings for every surface from the most knowledgeable and service oriented paint people.
AT THE TOP OF RAPHUNE HILL, ST. THOMAS, VIRGIN ISLANDS. 775-1466

MORE BRAINS THAN MONEY.

You can always find people with more money than brains. But, more brains than money?
Well, we see these people in our store every day. These people know the value of a dollar,
understand quality and truly appreciate top notch service.
When you need paint, shop where the smart money goes.

THE PAINT DEPOT

Coatings for every surface from the most knowledgeable and service oriented paint people.
AT THE TOP OF RAPHUNE HILL, ST. THOMAS, VIRGIN ISLANDS. 775-1466

DO YOU KNOW WHAT HAPPENS WHEN YOU COAT GALVANIZED METAL WITH AN ALKYD PAINT?

It's not your job to know, it's ours. Which is why we ask you so many questions. We want to make sure that you get the right coating, one that will be compatible with the surface. We'll ask you the condition of your walls or roof so we can recommend the right primer if required. Because the only time we want to see you back here in the near future is for one reason only: you want to change the color.

(P.S. If you paint raw galvanized metal with an alkyd paint, it'll peel off within 4 months. But don't worry, we've got the right primer for you.)

THE PAINT DEPOT

Coatings for every surface from the most knowledgeable and service oriented paint people.

AT THE TOP OF RAPHUNE HILL, ST. THOMAS, VIRGIN ISLANDS. 775-1466

FREE PAINT!

Now that you've seen the fine print, read the large print. Yes, we are giving away free paint.
Here's the deal. We have about 35 gallons of mistinted paint. The paint is perfectly good, you just have
to like the color. Limit: 1 free gallon per customer. All we ask is that you buy
something, even if it's only a $1.00 paint brush.
But hurry. Offer ends March 2, 2007

THE PAINT DEPOT
Coatings for every surface from the most knowledgeable and service oriented paint people.
AT THE TOP OF RAPHUNE HILL, ST. THOMAS, VIRGIN ISLANDS. 775-1466

Sometimes you can play with the typeface to add emphasis to your message.

IT'S TIME TO PLAN AHEAD

Every year you tell yourself "I'm going to plan ahead and prepare my roof for the hurricane season". And then you wait until it's too late and the rainy season begins. NOW is the time to just do it! We have everything you need to patch, repair and coat your roof. Use the Vulkem Urethane system for flat roofs and our ToughKote roof coating for your pitched roof. Plus, here's something that will stop your procrastination: our ToughKote water-based roof coating costs $48.00 LESS THAN the other leading brand. At these prices, we better plan ahead ourselves and order a lot more roof coating!

THE PAINT DEPOT

Coatings for every surface from the most knowledgeable and service oriented paint people.

AT THE TOP OF RAPHUNE HILL, ST. THOMAS, VIRGIN ISLANDS. 775-1466

HOW MANY PEOPLE DOES IT TAKE TO PAINT A SMALL BEDROOM?

Nine people.
First, there's you to apply the paint and then The Paint Depot with its eight staff members
to give you the right product, incredible service and a low price.

THE PAINT DEPOT

Coatings for every surface from the most knowledgeable and service oriented paint people.
AT THE TOP OF RAPHUNE HILL, ST. THOMAS, VIRGIN ISLANDS. 775-1466

HUE AND IMPROVED

We completely redid the area where you select your paint colors.
We have nice bar stools to sit on, a long and wide counter so you can spread out all those color cards.
After all, when it comes to the best color selection, we always have hue and you in mind.
Last, but not least, we revamped the entire store to make it easier for your to shop.
Why do all this? Because we believe the world should revolve around you.

THE PAINT DEPOT

Coatings for every surface from the most knowledgeable and service oriented paint people.
AT THE TOP OF RAPHUNE HILL, ST. THOMAS, VIRGIN ISLANDS. 775-1466

MARTIN-SENOUR PAINT. PURDY BRUSHES. WOOSTER ROLLERS. TOUGHKOTE ROOF COATINGS. WILREM URETHANE ROOF COATING. BENJAMIN MOORE PAINT. DYNAMIC ROLLERS. PAINT TRAYS. AUTOMOTIVE FINISHES. ZINSSER PRIMERS. RAMUC POOL PAINT. DAP SPACKLING. MINWAX STAINS. HELMSMAN VARNISH. GRACO AIRLESS SPRAYERS. PERMA WHITE MILDEW PROOF PAINT. GREAT OUTDOORS DECK STAIN. EUCOSEAL CISTERN COATING. H&C CON-CRETE STAIN. WERNER LADDERS. CARBOLINE INDUCTRIAL COATINGS.

When it's this crowded in here, it means we have everything that you could possibly need.

THE PAINT DEPOT

Coatings for every surface from the most knowledgeable and service oriented paint people.

AT THE TOP OF RAPHUNE HILL, ST. THOMAS, VIRGIN ISLANDS. 775-1466

I really did have a neighbor whose last name was Hebert. I made up my cousin Siskel though.

"THESE GUYS *REALLY* KNOW PAINT! TWO THUMBS UP!"

Siskel and Hebert
(That's Peter Siskel, my cousin and Don Hebert, my neighbor.)

THE PAINT DEPOT

Coatings for every surface from the most knowledgeable and service oriented paint people.
AT THE TOP OF RAPHUNE HILL, ST. THOMAS, VIRGIN ISLANDS. 775-1466

"GO AHEAD, MAKE MY DAY!"

Alright, here goes...
Our ToughKote water-based NSF P151 approved roof coating sells for $148.95 for gallons.
That's about *$30.00 less* than the other leading roof coating brand.

THE PAINT DEPOT

Coatings for every surface from the most knowledgeable and service oriented paint people.
AT THE TOP OF RAPHUNE HILL, ST. THOMAS, VIRGIN ISLANDS. 775-1466

Here's another ad we run during local elections.

BEN 'JAMMIN' MOORE RE-ELECTED BY A LANDSLIDE!

Once again, the voters have chosen
Ben "Jammin" Moore to be the official Paint Commissioner
for St. Thomas and St. John. This most colorful character will
continue to provide you with the best prices on paint and the
most incredible service. So, to celebrate his victory, he's putting
all Benjamin Moore brand paints on sale.
Plus he's lowering the price on all paint accessories
from 10% to 40% off until December 7th.
Visit his constituency office located at
The Paint Depot, Al Cohen Plaza,
St. Thomas, Virgin Islands.
You can call him anytime at 775-1466.

This ad paid for by the "Re-elect Ben "Jammin" Moore Committee"
(Also known as The Paint Depot)

THE PAINT DEPOT
Coatings for every surface from the most knowledgeable and service oriented paint people.
AT THE TOP OF RAPHUNE HILL, ST. THOMAS, VIRGIN ISLANDS. 775-1466

WORDS WE LIVE BY EVERYDAY.
(EXCEPT SUNDAY)

Take a moment and read the words located between the words THE PAINT DEPOT and the address line. Good. It's there every week but probably don't notice them. They are the words we live by every day, except Sunday of course, because we're closed then.

THE PAINT DEPOT

Coatings for every surface from the most knowledgeable and service oriented paint people.
AT THE TOP OF RAPHUNE HILL, ST. THOMAS, VIRGIN ISLANDS. 775-1466

GET WIND OF THIS.

If your house faces the trade winds directly, then you just might want a coating that will resist wind driven rain up to 98 mph...Stretchcoat Acrylic Elastomeric. It will resist peeling, flaking, cracking, chipping and mildew. It stays extremely flexible, can be applied thick and will cover hairline cracks.
The regular price for a 5 gallon pail is $119. but until July 19th, you can get it for only $83.30, that's 30% off!
But hurry, at this price, it's blowing out our doors.

THE PAINT DEPOT

Coatings for every surface from the most knowledgeable and service oriented paint people.
AT THE TOP OF RAPHUNE HILL, ST. THOMAS, VIRGIN ISLANDS. 775-1466

YOU'D BETTER HURRY

OUR BIGGEST SALE EVER FADES AWAY JULY 5TH.

THE PAINT DEPOT

Coatings for every surface from the most knowledgeable and service oriented paint people.
AT THE TOP OF RAPHUNE HILL, ST. THOMAS, VIRGIN ISLANDS. 775-1466

ARE YOU INTO M & S?

If you like kinky colors, the M & S (that's Martin-Senour paint) color chart is for you.
We've got "au naturel", "femme fatale", "exotic plum", "leather boot", "blue muse"
and "provacative plum". (Yes, these are all real color names.)
So, don't be shy. Come in and let's start a colorful affair.

THE PAINT DEPOT

Coatings for every surface from the most knowledgeable and service oriented paint people.
AT THE TOP OF RAPHUNE HILL, ST. THOMAS, VIRGIN ISLANDS. 775-1466

IT'S A "NO KNOW".

When you come into our store with a paint problem, we can usually solve it on the spot. Sometimes, however, it's a particularly tough coating problem that we just can't come up with an answer for. We call that a "no know". But don't worry. Leave your paint or roof coating problem with us and we'll do some research to get you an answer.
Because around here, not solving your problem is a definite "no, no".

THE PAINT DEPOT

Coatings for every surface from the most knowledgeable and service oriented paint people.
AT THE TOP OF RAPHUNE HILL, ST. THOMAS, VIRGIN ISLANDS. 775-1466

2 + 2 = 5

Buy 4 gallons of ToughKote elastomeric roof coating and get the fifth gallon free.
Offer valid March 10-17. Cash sales only.

THE PAINT DEPOT

Coatings for every surface from the most knowledgeable and service oriented paint people.

AT THE TOP OF RAPHUNE HILL, ST. THOMAS, VIRGIN ISLANDS. 775-1466

I HAVE BAD NEWS.

But first the good news. All Martin-Senour Great Life exterior latex paints are 20% off.
This is our premium quality paint.
And now for the bad news. Sales ends April 21.

THE PAINT DEPOT

Coatings for every surface from the most knowledgeable and service oriented paint people.
AT THE TOP OF RAPHUNE HILL, ST. THOMAS, VIRGIN ISLANDS. 775-1466

IF YOU BELIEVE THE WORLD SHOULD REVOLVE AROUND YOU, THEN YOU'VE COME TO THE RIGHT PLACE.

THE PAINT DEPOT

Coatings for every surface from the most knowledgeable and service oriented paint people.

AT THE TOP OF RAPHUNE HILL, ST. THOMAS, VIRGIN ISLANDS. 775-1466

These ads ran a week apart. It took some effort to decode the message as it was in Morse Code. We received about three dozen entries.

SECRET CODE

The first three people (one per household), who call in and tell me what this code says exactly, will each win $100.00 cash. So why am I doing this? It's the only thing I could come up with for an ad this week.
(When you call, ask for Mike. You have until March 2, 2007)

".. ...-. / -.-- --- ..- / -.... .-. ..- .... . / - .... / .-- --- -.-. ..-./ ... . --- ..-. -.
-. . ..-- --- ...-..- ./ .-. .-.-- ...-.-./ -.-- --- ..-/ - .... .-./ -.-- --- ... ../ -.-. --- .
. --- / - .... ./ -.. ...--. .... - / .-- .-.-. -.. ."

THE PAINT DEPOT
Coatings for every surface from the most knowledgeable and service oriented paint people.
AT THE TOP OF RAPHUNE HILL, ST. THOMAS, VIRGIN ISLANDS. 775-1466

DOT DASH DOT DOT

(Answer to the Secret Code ad that ran in the Daily News last Monday. Congrats to our winners!)

*If you believe
the world should revolve around you,
then you've come to the right place.*

THE PAINT DEPOT

Coatings for every surface from the most knowledgeable and service oriented paint people.

AT THE TOP OF RAPHUNE HILL, ST. THOMAS, VIRGIN ISLANDS. 775-1466

"YELLOW, THIS IS THE PAINT DEPOT!"

You know you live and breathe paint colors when you start answering the phone like this.

THE PAINT DEPOT

Coatings for every surface from the most knowledgeable and service oriented paint people.
AT THE TOP OF RAPHUNE HILL, ST. THOMAS, VIRGIN ISLANDS. 775-1466

BEST OF AD.

We've won Best Paint Store every year except one. Best Customer Service is chosen among ALL retail store categories (jewelry, department stores, grocery, etc) in the Virgin Islands. We won that category six times.

WHO'S THE BIGGEST WINNER? OUR CUSTOMERS!

Best Paint Store 2001
Best Paint Store 2002
Best Paint Store 2003
Best Paint Store 2004
Best Paint Store 2005
Best Paint Store 2006
Best Paint Store 2007
Best Paint Store 2008
Best Paint Store 2009
Best Customer Service 2009
Best Paint Store 2010
Best Paint Store 2011
Best Paint Store 2012
Best Paint Store 2013
Best Customer Service 2013
Best Paint Store 2015
Best Paint Store 2016
Best Customer Service 2016
Best Paint Store 2017
Best Paint Store 2018
Best Paint Store 2019
Best Customer Service 2019
Best Paint Store 2020
Best Customer Service 2020
Best Paint Store 2021
Best Customer Service 2021

You don't win this many times unless you're doing <u>everything</u> right for your customers. For 27 years, The Paint Depot team has been giving the absolute best paint and roof coating advice in the Virgin Islands.
Come in and let us treat you like a somebody!

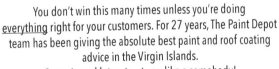

THE PAINT DEPOT
ST. THOMAS, VIRGIN ISLANDS. 775-1466

WISE EXTRAVAGANCE.

When painting the exterior of your home it doesn't cost much more to get the very best quality paint.
Now, we've got inexpensive paints as well, but when you're painting exterior surfaces, two paints of paint
(which is only about .004 inches thick) is suppose to protect your home from the salt air, the tropical sun
and strong wind driven rain. With our Great Life exterior 100% acrylic latex flat paint, you'll be
getting the best quality coating for your walls for only $24.26 a gallon.
An inexpensive indulgence for the best coat for your home.

THE PAINT DEPOT

Coatings for every surface from the most knowledgeable and service oriented paint people.
AT THE TOP OF RAPHUNE HILL, ST. THOMAS, VIRGIN ISLANDS. 775-1466

THANKS FOR GIVING.

As our way of saying "Thanks For Giving" us your business, we'd like to offer you great prices on everything in the store.
All Martin Senour paints from 20% to 50% off! All paint accessories from 10% to 40% off!
Dap spackle, 1 gallon reg. $19.95, NOW $12.76! Polyseamseal acrylic latex caulk with silicone, 10 oz tube, reg. $2.75 NOW $1.47!
ToughKote flashing, 5 gal, reg. $129.00 NOW $96.75!

Sale ends December 7. Cash sales only.

THE PAINT DEPOT

Coatings for every surface from the most knowledgeable and service oriented paint people.
AT THE TOP OF RAPHUNE HILL, ST. THOMAS, VIRGIN ISLANDS. 775-1466

IF YOUR LIFE *ACTUALLY* DEPENDED ON THE PERFECT PAINT COLOR MATCH, WHERE WOULD YOU GO?

The Paint Depot. Saving perfect color match lives since 1995.

THE PAINT DEPOT

Coatings for every surface from the most knowledgeable and service oriented paint people.
AT THE TOP OF RAPHUNE HILL, ST. THOMAS, VIRGIN ISLANDS. 775-1466

"DADDY, WHERE DO ALL THE TROPICAL FISH GET THEIR COLORS FROM?"

They get all their colors from right here.

THE PAINT DEPOT

Coatings for every surface from the most knowledgeable and service oriented paint people.

AT THE TOP OF RAPHUNE HILL, ST. THOMAS, VIRGIN ISLANDS. 775-1466

WHY ARE YOU ASKING ME ALL THESE QUESTIONS?

When you come to buy paint from us, we're going to ask you a bunch of questions. We want to make sure that you get the right coating, one that will be compatible with the surface it's going on. We'll ask you the condition of your walls or roof so we can recommend the right primer if required. Because the only time we want to see you back here in the near future is for one reason only: you what to change the color.

THE PAINT DEPOT

Coatings for every surface from the most knowledgeable and service oriented paint people.

AT THE TOP OF RAPHUNE HILL, ST. THOMAS, VIRGIN ISLANDS. 775-1466

IN ONE WORD
DESCRIBE THE SERVICE HERE.

Supercalifragilisticexpialidotious!

THE PAINT DEPOT
Coatings for every surface from the most knowledgeable and service oriented paint people.
AT THE TOP OF RAPHUNE HILL, ST. THOMAS, VIRGIN ISLANDS. 775-1466

INSIDE JOB.

If you're ready to paint the inside of your house, then here's your chance to get a real steal on our Proline Supreme Interior latex semi-gloss paint.
This stuff is regularly priced at $99.95 for a 5 gallon pail but you can get it right now for $74.96!
That's 25% off! Don't put it off.

THE PAINT DEPOT

Coatings for every surface from the most knowledgeable and service oriented paint people.
AT THE TOP OF RAPHUNE HILL, ST. THOMAS, VIRGIN ISLANDS. 775-1466

"AND THE NOMINEES FOR BEST PERFORMANCE IN A PAINT FILM ARE..."

"Benjamin-Moore, Martin-Senour and Zinsser Paint!"
To get your ticket to the toughest, most beautiful paint film for your home,
direct yourself to our color studio.

THE PAINT DEPOT

Coatings for every surface from the most knowledgeable and service oriented paint people.
AT THE TOP OF RAPHUNE HILL, ST. THOMAS, VIRGIN ISLANDS. 775-1466

VENI. MERCABILIS. ARDORIS.

Translation: I came. I shopped. I loved it.

When in Rome, you do as the Romans do.
So when you need paint, you come to the place with the most
variety of coatings---from roof to cisterns to cars. Inside and outside. For homes and industry.
It's all here including exceptional service.

THE PAINT DEPOT

Coatings for every surface from the most knowledgeable and service oriented paint people.
AT THE TOP OF RAPHUNE HILL, ST. THOMAS, VIRGIN ISLANDS. 775-1466

DECK THE HALLS,

And have a Happy Holiday from your friends
Bobby, Dwayne, Ernest, Kirsty, Mark, Mike and Linda.

THE PAINT DEPOT

Coatings for every surface from the most knowledgeable and service oriented paint people.
AT THE TOP OF RAPHUNE HILL, ST. THOMAS, VIRGIN ISLANDS. 775-1466

TICK, TICK, TICK,

Tick.
Time is running out on our biggest sale ever!
Every paint, every brush, every roller, every "thing" is on sale at up to 40% off.

THE PAINT DEPOT
Coatings for every surface from the most knowledgeable and service oriented paint people.
AT THE TOP OF RAPHUNE HILL, ST. THOMAS, VIRGIN ISLANDS. 775-1466

"I DON'T NEED PAINT!"

Even if you don't need paint right now, you'll want to buy some from us. Because at up to 40% off, painting has never been easier or more affordable. Take our Platinum Exterior eggshell finish latex, reg. $27.95, NOW $18.16, save 35%! Or Great Life exterior semi-gloss, reg. $24.95, NOW $17.46 a gallon, save 30%! Ralph Lauren paints, limited quantities, all at 40% off!
Yeah, I know. *Now* you want paint.

THE PAINT DEPOT

Coatings for every surface from the most knowledgeable and service oriented paint people.
AT THE TOP OF RAPHUNE HILL, ST. THOMAS, VIRGIN ISLANDS. 775-1466

In this sale, we used Scratch'N'Win
cards for the prizes.

IF YOU SCRATCH MINE,
I'LL SCRATCH YOURS.

Buy any Martin-Senour paint (you'll be scratching my back) and you get a 'Scratch'n'Win' card (that's me scratching yours).
Every card is a winner. Could be a key chain, could be a mini stereo, could be a free movie. Could be one of 500 prizes.
But no matter what you win, you'll be ahead in more ways than one. Great paint, excellent price,
incredible service and something free with each purchase. Offer ends February 3, 2001.

THE PAINT DEPOT

Coatings for every surface from the most knowledgeable and service oriented paint people.
AT THE TOP OF RAPHUNE HILL, ST. THOMAS, VIRGIN ISLANDS. 775-1466

THE END IS NEAR!

The end of the biggest paint sale on island ends May 31, so hurry!
Savings up to 35% off everything in the store!
Don't be grim, reap the rewards now!

THE PAINT DEPOT

Coatings for every surface from the most knowledgeable and service oriented paint people.
AT THE TOP OF RAPHUNE HILL, ST. THOMAS, VIRGIN ISLANDS. 775-1466

PAINT BY NUMBERS.

1. Martin Senour ProLine Premium ext. latex s/g, 1 gal. was $19.95, the number is now $14.96!
2. Martin Senour Proline Premium int. e/g latex, 1 gal. was $17.95, the number is now $13.46!
3. Martin Senour Porch and Floor enamel, latex, 1 gal. was $26.95, the number is now $17.51!
4. Martin Senour Stretchcoat Elastomeric paint, 5 gal. was $119.00, the number is now $95.20!
5. We have 3,259 other items on sale at up to 35% off. Sale ends May 31.

THE PAINT DEPOT

Coatings for every surface from the most knowledgeable and service oriented paint people.

AT THE TOP OF RAPHUNE HILL, ST. THOMAS, VIRGIN ISLANDS. 775-1466

LESS MONEY. MORE PAINT.

Martin Senour's Platinum paints have less water in each gallon. So, what's in it instead? More solids, more mildewcide, more guts for better hiding power. As a matter of fact, up to 20% more ingredients than other national brand paints. If you're looking for the finest paint available, then get Martin Senour's Platinum interior and exterior paints.
And until March 18th, we'll give you 20% off the regular price.

THE PAINT DEPOT

Coatings for every surface from the most knowledgeable and service oriented paint people.
AT THE TOP OF RAPHUNE HILL, ST. THOMAS, VIRGIN ISLANDS. 775-1466

THE 'H' WORD.

I'm not even going to say the word.
But you know that with the "H" season officially here, we are going to start getting much more rain.
So, if you have a leak in your roof now, it doesn't take a genius to figure out it's only going to get worse. The time to fix, repair and recoat you roof is now, right now. We've got everything you need---Vulkem for flat roofs, ToughKote for pitched roofs (which by way costs about $30.00 less a pail than the "other" brand). We also have tape, brushes, rollers and sleeves.
And if you need someone to go up on your roof to offer a recommendation, we'll be glad to do that. For free.
After all, isn't that what you would expect from the most knowledgeable and service oriented people.

THE PAINT DEPOT

Coatings for every surface from the most knowledgeable and service oriented paint people.
AT THE TOP OF RAPHUNE HILL, ST. THOMAS, VIRGIN ISLANDS. 775-1466

WE'D LIKE TO FILM YOUR HOUSE.

With Martin Senour or Benjamin Moore paint film of course.
You'll get the toughest, most beautiful paint film anywhere. So direct yourself to The Paint Depot
where you'll find great products, incredible service *and* low prices.

THE PAINT DEPOT

Coatings for every surface from the most knowledgeable and service oriented paint people.
AT THE TOP OF RAPHUNE HILL, ST. THOMAS, VIRGIN ISLANDS. 775-1466

TO ALL THE PEOPLE WHO DON'T BUY THEIR PAINT HERE.

If you're into saving money, then come in here and buy a barbecue basting brush. Huh? Just bear with me. The other day I was in a grocery store and saw a 2" china bristle basting brush for $2.99. We sell those exact same 2" bristle brushes for .90 cents! So if you're wondering why you would drive all the way here for a .90 cent brush to baste your chicken, other than the fact you'll save $2.09, I'll tell you. The absolute incredible service. Because even when you're just buying a basting brush, which, by the way, you can use for painting as well, you'll be treated like a somebody. And while you're here, you might as well check out our low paint prices.

THE PAINT DEPOT

Coatings for every surface from the most knowledgeable and service oriented paint people.

AT THE TOP OF RAPHUNE HILL, ST. THOMAS, VIRGIN ISLANDS. 775-1466

"AND THE WINNER FOR BEST SPECIAL EFFECTS IN A PAINT FILM IS..."

Pratt & Lambert Ovation Suede finish paint.

THE PAINT DEPOT

Coatings for every surface from the most knowledgeable and service oriented paint people.
AT THE TOP OF RAPHUNE HILL, ST. THOMAS, VIRGIN ISLANDS. 775-1466

ON THE NEXT PAGE, YOU WILL SEE A LIST OF **EVERY** ROOF COATING IN THE ENTIRE WORLD THAT CAN DO BOTH OF THESE THINGS...

1.
Have an official NSF P151 rating
for collecting drinking water from a roof.

2.
Can be used on flat roofs
with severe ponding water.

These full page ads ran on consecutive pages in the local newspaper.

VULKEM!

Vulkem has proven itself to be the most effective roof coating for flat roofs
for over a decade here in the Virgin Islands.
Over 2 million sq. ft. has been applied to homes, businesses, hotels,
government buildings and parking decks.
Vulkem works. Period.

SAFE. BETTER.

MUST BE VULKEM!

The Vulkem 450/451 system is the only liquid roof coating system available that is suitable for use on a flat roof with continuous ponding water <u>and</u> has the official NSF P151 certification. It is the toughest, most stringent test for collecting safe drinking water for your cistern.

That's why you'll find Vulkem used at schools, hospitals, government buildings, hotels, retail stores and homes.
The Vulkem Urethane roofing system has been applied to over two million square feet of surfaces in the Virgin Islands.
It has more adhesive strength, more tensile strength, more waterproofing ability than *any water-based roof coating!*

So, if you haven't found a solution to your leaky roof,
then do what property owners, architects and contractors do...THEY VULKEM IT!

THE PAINT DEPOT

Coatings for every surface from the most knowledgeable and service oriented paint people.
AT THE TOP OF RAPHUNE HILL, ST. THOMAS, VIRGIN ISLANDS. 775-1466

PAINT DEPOT T-SHIRTS.

This is the back of our T-shirts. It covers the whole area. The front has a small logo. We give away over 500 a year.

We've only sold our T shirts once. That was after 9/11. We had 750 of them printed up with the words True Colors and the American flag on the front. We raised $7,000. which was donated to an agency in New York City.

THE
PAINT
DEPOT
N 18° W 64°

We're all here because we're not all there!

Valentine's Day is a big thing in the Virgin Islands. We run this ad a week or two prior to the event.

ROSES ARE RED, VIOLETS ARE BLUE, WE'LL MIX YOUR PAINT, IN ANY HUE.

If you're looking to impress, and I mean really impress your significant other, then surprise them this Valentine's Day by painting a room in their favorite color. Flowers will wilt in a few days but our Benjamin Moore colors will stay vibrant for a very, very long time.

THE PAINT DEPOT

Coatings for every surface from the most knowledgeable and service oriented paint people.
AT THE TOP OF RAPHUNE HILL, ST. THOMAS, VIRGIN ISLANDS. 775-1466

FUND RAISING.

This is one of the ads we ran to raise money for the victims of the tsunami in South-East Asia.

HELP US SEND A WAVE OF RELIEF!

We were giving away these extremely popular, heavy duty canvas bags to our customers as Christmas gifts. But now, I'm going to ask you to give me $18.00 for them.

Every single dollar we collect from the sale of these canvas bags will be sent to help the families of the Tsunami disaster in South-East Asia.

If you buy ten or more, I'll personally deliver them to your place of work.

I've seen these exact bags for sale online for $19.95, so at $18.00, you're not only getting a good deal

These 100% cotton, heavy duty canvas bags have antique brass tumbuckles, an inside hanging zippered pocket and a large front flap. But the best part about the purchase of this rugged shoulder bag is that every dollar we collect will go to help the families of the tsunami disaster in South-East Asia.

and a very practical canvas bag, but you'll be helping people who now have to cope with the aftermath of one of the largest natural disasters ever to hit the planet.

The canvas bags are available here at The Paint Depot. If you can't come in, call with your Visa or Mastercard and we'll mail it to you for an extra $3.00 each to cover shipping.

Time is truly of the essence. Help us send a huge wave of relief.

Thank you.
(All proceeds will be sent to AmeriCares Foundation. You can visit their web site at www.americares.org)

THE PAINT DEPOT
AL COHEN PLAZA, ST. THOMAS, VIRGIN ISLANDS. 775-1466

CHIGAGO: $29.95
NEW YORK: $28.95
MIAMI: $28.50

BUT IN ST. THOMAS $27.95!

Yes, everything costs more in the Virgin Islands.
Except for us.
I called some Benjamin Moore dealers in Chicago, New York
and Miami and asked how much for a gallon of
Benjamin Moore Moorguard exterior latex flat paint.
And surprise! We sell that same gallon for *less* than they do.
And we have to ship our paint down here by boat!
So, yes, you might pay more for stuff in St. Thomas
but you can make up for some of it by shopping here.

THE PAINT DEPOT
Coatings for every surface from the most knowledgeable and service oriented paint people.
AT THE TOP OF RAPHUNE HILL, ST. THOMAS, VIRGIN ISLANDS. 775-1466

QUANTIFY!

Things cost more in the Virgin Islands. That's because we have to ship everything to Miami and then ship it by boat to the island. Or does it?

I called some paint stores in a few big cities and was suprised that our prices were better on this particular paint.

So we took advantage of the price difference in this ad.

Quantify! To have said our prices are better than the other guy would have been lame. But comparing actual prices, the message becomes believable.

HOW WILL I END THIS BOOK?

When I was thinking of an ending for this book
I decided to play, 'what if'?

What if instead of opening up a paint store,
I opened up a different business.

So, I changed the name "Paint" to different kinds of businesses
and started writing ads in the same vein using the same design elements.

Creativity is setting your mind free of constraints.
You need to make ridiculous associations and just go with it.
These are irreverant but fun. Hope you enjoy them.

Mike Perron
St. Thomas, Virgin Islands.

PETITS

We carry all sizes of bras including small and extra small.

THE LINGERIE DEPOT

AT THE TOP OF RAPHUNE HILL, ST. THOMAS, VIRGIN ISLANDS. 775-1466

MAN EATING FISH!

...woman eating octopus..

...Sashimi, nigiri, uni, eel, California rolls and other delicious sushi selections which can be found daily at...

THE SUSHI DEPOT

AT THE TOP OF RAPHUNE HILL, ST. THOMAS, VIRGIN ISLANDS. 775-1466

BEWARE OF GEEKS BEARING GIFS!

Got a Trojan Horse virus in your computer?
Then giddyap over here and we'll take care of it pronto!

THE COMPUTER DEPOT

AT THE TOP OF RAPHUNE HILL, ST. THOMAS, VIRGIN ISLANDS. 775-1466

"IT TASTED LIKE ANGELS COPULATING ON MY TONGUE!"

Chateau Mouton-Rothschild, 2016.
(We carry only the finest wines to amuse your taste buds.)

THE WINE DEPOT

AT THE TOP OF RAPHUNE HILL, ST. THOMAS, VIRGIN ISLANDS. 775-1466

THE FECES IMPINGED ON THE OCSILATING BLADES.

Got a public relations problem?
Call us. We know how to say it nicely

THE PR DEPOT
AT THE TOP OF RAPHUNE HILL, ST. THOMAS, VIRGIN ISLANDS. 775-1466

KISS YOUR HEMORRHOIDS GOODBYE.

We have everything to help get rid of that pain in the you know what.
You'll find it in aisle H.

THE PHARMACY DEPOT

AT THE TOP OF RAPHUNE HILL, ST. THOMAS, VIRGIN ISLANDS. 775-1466

"I'M AS HUNGRY AS JEFFREY DAHMER."

Would you like a leg or a thigh?

THE FRIED CHICKEN DEPOT

AT THE TOP OF RAPHUNE HILL, ST. THOMAS, VIRGIN ISLANDS. 775-1466

OINKMENT

Specially formulated anti aging face cream made with real bacon fat.

THE COSMETICS DEPOT

AT THE TOP OF RAPHUNE HILL, ST. THOMAS, VIRGIN ISLANDS. 775-1466

CUNNING LINGUIST.

Learn to be assertive *and* acquire a second language all in one course.
This will help you get the job you want at the CIA.

THE LANGUAGE DEPOT

AT THE TOP OF RAPHUNE HILL, ST. THOMAS, VIRGIN ISLANDS. 775-1466

EITHER WAY YOU GET YOUR DOG BACK.

THE VETERINARY & TAXIDERMY DEPOT

AT THE TOP OF RAPHUNE HILL, ST. THOMAS, VIRGIN ISLANDS. 775-1466

NEED MONEY TO BRIBE SOMEONE?

We'll loan you some money so you can bribe *yourself* through the inconveniences of life. Like a broken air conditioner or a set of new tires. Come in and let us slip you some money.

THE LOAN DEPOT

AT THE TOP OF RAPHUNE HILL, ST. THOMAS, VIRGIN ISLANDS. 775-1466

THE END.

That means it's time to pick up your next book!
We've got all the latest titles in stock.

THE BOOK DEPOT

AT THE TOP OF RAPHUNE HILL, ST. THOMAS, VIRGIN ISLANDS. 775-1466